W9-BGM-425

The Other Battle
of
The Bulge

Operation Northwind

THE OTHER BATTLE OF THE BULGE

OPERATION *NORTHWIND*

by

Charles Whiting

CASEMATE
Havertown, PA

Published by
CASEMATE
2114 Darby Road, Havertown, PA 19083

Copyright © 1986, 1990, 2002 by Charles Whiting

All rights reserved. No part of this publication
may be reproduced, stored in a retrieval system or transmitted
in any form or by any means, electronic, mechanical,
photocopying, recording or otherwise,
without prior permission in writing from the Publishers.

ISBN 0-9711709-7-5

Cataloging-in-publication data is available from the
Library of Congress

Also published in the United Kingdom in 2002 by
Spellmount Ltd, The Old Rectory, Staplehurst, Kent TN12 0AZ
ISBN 1-86227-122-4

1 3 5 7 9 8 6 4 2

Manufactured in Great Britain

CONTENTS

DEDICATION

Above all, I should like to thank the men who were there that terrible winter, Mr Hy Schorr and Mr Tom Dickinson of New York City. Without their help *Operation Northwind* could not have been written. I should also like to dedicate this book to those young men of the 3rd, 28th, 36th, 42nd, 44th, 45th, 63rd, 70th, 75th, 79th, 100th, and 103rd Infantry Divisions, the 101st Airborne Division and their comrades of the 12th and 14th Armored Divisions. Sixty odd years ago now, they sailed away from the shores of the United States, full of youthful energy and confidence, to 'liberate' France. To those many thousand who never returned, this book is humbly dedicated.

Charles Whiting

The map entitled "The Battle of Alsace" is reproduced from Forrest C Pogue's *The Supreme Command*, U.S. Army in World War II, (Washington, D.C.: Government Printing Office, 1954), courtesy U.S. Army Center of Military History.

Photographs are reprinted courtesy of the U.S. National Archives and General Research Division, the New York Public Library, Astor, Lenox and Tilden Foundations.

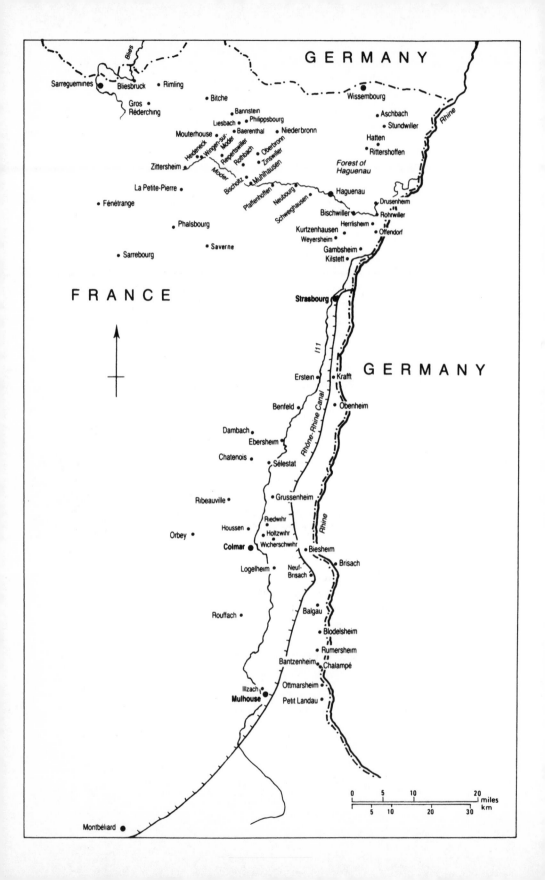

INTRODUCTION

The Battle of the Bulge, the German surprise attack on the American lines in the Belgian Ardennes in December, 1944, is celebrated in American military history as the major battle fought by the US Army in Europe in the Second World War.

Books on the subject, fiction and non-fiction, would fill a small library. It has been depicted in half a dozen films and a score of TV documentaries. Not many years ago the Battle of the Bulge was again world news, due to President Reagan's controversial visit to Bitburg cemetery, Germany, where some of the SS who murdered US prisoners near Malmedy during the battle supposedly lie buried. Every high school kid can quote General MacAuliffe's scornful reply to the German offer to surrender when his division was surrounded by them at Bastogne, 'Nuts'. Actually he snorted something much cruder. Fortunately for the legend, his PR man censored the expletive in time. It could hardly have appeared in a school history book.

But who knows that the man who commanded the 'battered bastards of Bastogne' during that celebrated siege went on to command another division in a second Battle of the Bulge? Who knows, too, that nearly a thousand of those airborne troopers who had survived the fight at Bastogne were either killed or wounded in that second battle, without benefit of publicity or the media coverage their earlier stand had gained them? The history of that second Battle of the Bulge in the winter of 1944/45 has never been recorded, in spite of the fact that it lasted a month longer than the original Battle of the Bulge and cost the Americans some 16,000 casualties. It also cost perhaps twice that number of French soldiers serving under American command.

Yet, strategically and politically, it was a much more significant battle than the original Battle of the Bulge. It can be argued that if the Germans' second attack *had* succeeded, the whole Western military alliance might have broken up and France been plunged into political anarchy. Indeed, although the German plan did not succeed, the bitter memories of that second Battle of the Bulge had a long-term influence on Franco-American relations: one which, in the end, probably led to General de Gaulle's decision to leave NATO and ensure that the defence of France lay solely in the hands of Frenchmen.

As we shall see, that unknown battle also first brought the United States Army indirectly into contact with an area and a problem which three decades later would escalate into America's most significant military defeat of the second half of the twentieth century – Vietnam.

What was this unknown battle? It was a German attack which the American command, thanks to Ultra, knew was coming. Yet it was one, too, which dealt them a stunning blow and forced the Supreme Commander, General Eisenhower, to order the first and only retreat of an American army in the whole course of the campaign in Western Europe. The Führer himself had given the attack its code-name *Unternehmen Nordwind* – a bold assault on the apparently unsuspecting US Seventh Army dug in in the French border province of Alsace-Lorraine, just below the embattled Belgian Ardennes.

While the Americans were fully occupied in the north, warding off the attack in the Bulge, thinning their lines out to allow Patton's Third Army to counterattack, this new offensive would completely surprise the Americans in France, recapture Alsace-Lorraine and, with a bit of luck, knock France out of the war.

Thus it was, as the quarter of a million GIs of General Alexander Patch's relatively green US Seventh Army prepared to celebrate the last New Year's Eve of the Second World War, eight German divisions, three of them SS, readied themselves in the snow-bound French hills for the surprise assault. At eleven-thirty precisely on the night of 31 December, 1944, that great wind would sweep down upon the *Amis* and Operation Northwind, the Second Battle of the Bulge, would begin.

A Call to Arms

'We can still lose this war,'
General George Patton, 4 January, 1945

On Tuesday, 19 December, 1944, the Top Brass converged on the town of Verdun – Verdun, an ominously evocative name, where in the First World War hundreds of thousands of Frenchmen and Germans had been slaughtered. Adolf Hitler had been wounded on those barren ridges which overlooked the town. De Gaulle had been captured there. In 1916 the fate of France had hung in the balance as Germany seemed set on breaking through at Verdun and winning the war.

Now on this cold grey morning, as the Top Brass filed into the squad room at the eighteenth-century barracks, Maginot Caserne, the situation appeared little different. Three days before, the Germans had launched another great attack in the Belgian Ardennes which had caught the Western Allies completely by surprise. Just as at Verdun twenty-eight years before, it had smashed through the American lines in the Ardennes, sending the divisions holding the front there reeling back in disarray. Now, as the clock in the Vauban citadel down in the town began to strike eleven, the Germans fifty miles away were racing for the River Meuse. Beyond that lay their key objectives, the great Allied supply port of Antwerp and Brussels itself.

Shivering in the squalid room, heated by a single pot-bellied stove, the Top Brass took their places, their staffs behind them. All were important men who commanded the destinies of hundreds of thousands, even millions, of soldiers, British, American, Canadian, French, and a dozen other nationalities. But this morning, as the bad news from the front mounted, they seemed powerless to act. Everything now rested in the hands of the Supreme Commander, General Eisenhower.

His Chief-of-Intelligence, General Strong, recalled many years later,

'The meeting was crowded and the atmosphere tense. The British were worried by events. As so often before, their confidence in the ability of Americans to deal with the situation was not great. Reports had been reaching them of disorganization behind the American lines, of American headquarters abandoned without notice, and of documents and weapons falling intact into enemy hands. Stories of great bravery on the part of individuals and units did not change their opinion.'[1]

The Verdun Conference, as it became known, was perhaps the high point of Eisenhower's career as Supreme Commander in Europe. His front had been virtually torn in half. Against all the confident predictions of his top intelligence men, who had maintained for the last month that the Germans were beaten – 'vying with each other for the honor of devastating the German war machine with words', as Robert E. Merriam of the US 9th Army put it[2] – the enemy had launched a major counterattack.

Even if the Germans only succeeded in crossing the River Meuse, would this not mean the end of the confidence the public had placed in the Supreme Commander since the triumphant D-Day landings? Although Eisenhower knew he enjoyed the powerful protection of General Marshall back in Washington, he was too much of a realist not to realize that he had mighty enemies in the Allied camp, especially in Britain. Would they not be only too eager to accuse him of slackness, inefficiency, lack of foresight and worse?

It was not surprising, therefore, that when he entered that icy room, chain-smoking as always, his usual happy grin was absent. Instead, his broad face was pale and set. But, after he had looked around at Generals Bradley, Devers, Patton and the rest, he announced, 'The present situation is to be regarded as one of opportunity for us and not one of disaster.' He paused and forced a smile. 'There will be only cheerful faces at this conference table!' As always Patton, Commander of the US Third Army, was first off the mark. The remark appealed to his pugnacious, if somewhat flippant, nature. 'Hell, let's have the guts to let the sons of bitches go all the way to Paris. Then we'll really cut 'em off and show 'em up!'[3] The ice was broken. From that moment onwards it was Patton's conference. While Eisenhower crumpled a pack of Lucky Strike (he chain-smoked sixty a day), Brigadier Kenneth Strong sketched in the situation at the front. It was bad. The Germans had already committed twenty divisions in the Ardennes, five of them armoured. Intelligence knew that the enemy had plenty more divisions in reserve, which could be used in the Ardennes. But attacks elsewhere on the long front, stretching from Holland down to Switzerland, could not be ruled out either.

Bradley's front in the Ardennes had been split and his armies separated by the 'Bulge', as it was now being called. There was only one solution, if General Montgomery was not to be asked to come to the rescue (and all the American commanders were bitterly opposed to that): Patton must make a strong counterattack into the 'Bulge' from the south.

Following up Strong's exposé with a few words of his own, Eisenhower turned to Patton and said, 'George, I want you to go to Luxembourg and take charge of the battle, making a strong counter-attack with at least six divisions. When can you start?'

'As soon as you are through with me,' Patton answered in his usual brash manner.

According to Strong, 'There was some laughter around the table, especially from the British officers present.'[4] To them, it seemed a typical Patton reaction, rash and unrealistic. To achieve his aim, Patton would have to swing his Third Army around in a ninety-degree angle from their present positions in Lorraine and the Saar. This would mean moving *133,178 motor vehicles over 1.6 million road miles* in the worst winter Europe had experienced in a quarter of a century!

But Patton was undaunted by the prospect. 'I left my household in Nancy in perfect order before I came here,' he said triumphantly, pleased with the impression he had made. Eisenhower now looked more kindly on the man he had saved from being removed from his command at least twice in the last couple of years. 'When can you start?' he asked again.

'The morning of 22 December,' Patton answered without the slightest hesitation.

Colonel Codman, Patton's aide, recorded later that the reaction to that bold assurance was 'electric'. 'There was a stir, a shuffling of feet, as those present straightened up in their chairs. In some faces, scepticism. But through the room the current of excitement leaped like a flame.'[5]

'Don't be fatuous, George!' Eisenhower snapped severely.

Calmly Patton lit a cigar and said, 'This has nothing to do with being fatuous, sir. I've made my arrangements and my staff are working like beavers at this very moment to shape them up.'

Quickly he sketched in his plan of attack and then, turning to General Bradley, he exclaimed, 'Brad, this time the Kraut has stuck his head in a meat grinder.' He held up his fist clenched round the cigar. 'And this time I've got hold of the handle!'

The symbolism of the gesture wasn't lost on the others. There was laughter, and even Eisenhower grinned. Now the conference began to break up into separate discussion groups. Eisenhower strolled over to Patton just before he left and said, 'Funny thing, George, every time I get another star [Eisenhower had just been made five-star general], I get attacked.'

'Yeah,' Patton quipped, elated with his new task and very much the star. 'And every time you get attacked, I have to bail you out.'[6]

One year later, when Patton lay dying in the military hospital in Heidelberg, Eisenhower cabled him: 'Bradley has just [reminded] me that when we three met in Verdun to consider plans, you and your army were given vital missions. From that moment on our worries with respect to the battle began to disappear. Nothing could stop you, including storms, cold, snow-blocked roads and a savagely fighting enemy. We want you to know that in your present battle we are supremely confident that your spirit will again bring victory.'[7]

In all the accounts of that celebrated conference at Verdun, which helped to determine the course of the most important battle fought by the US Army in Europe in the Second World War, invariably most of the attention is focused on the star of the show, General Patton. But there was another general present that day whose men were going to play an equally decisive role in the coming events as those commanded by Patton. Indeed, it can be argued that if his troops had been defeated, not only would Patton's drive into the southern flank of the Bulge have failed, but the whole Western Alliance would have collapsed. That general was Jacob L. Devers, commander of the US 6th Army Group, consisting of the US Seventh Army and the French First Army, currently holding the line of the Upper Rhine from the Swiss border to a little north of Strasbourg.

Big, bald, and something of a bureaucrat, General 'Jake' Devers had been a classmate of Patton's at West Point. Like Patton, Devers was a cavalryman and a keen polo player (in 1931 Devers had captained the team, in which Patton also played, that won the Argentine Polo Cup for the USA). But there the similarity ended. Devers had seen little action and, as the only army commander *not* specifically recommended by Eisenhower for his appointment, he was regarded with some suspicion by the latter.

Prior to the invasion he and Eisenhower had fought a running battle. Devers insisted on holding on to commanders whom Eisenhower felt he needed for the coming battle. More than once Eisenhower had complained to General Marshall about Devers' lack of cooperation. Later, when Devers' armies attacked Southern France and began their four-month-long drive towards the German frontier and their link-up with the Allied troops attacking out of the Normandy bridgeheads, Eisenhower complained that Devers lacked command ability. Indeed, when asked by the US War Department to rate thirty-eight of his highest officers, Eisenhower placed Devers at twenty-four, lower than several humble corps commanders. Worse, he was the only officer of the whole thirty-eight of whom Eisenhower had something negative to report. Devers, he wrote to Washington, was 'often inaccurate in statements and evaluations. . . . He has not, so far, produced among the seniors of the American organization here a feeling of trust and confidence.'[8]

Among those in the know, it was generally supposed that the Supreme Commander retained Devers only because he hated removing lieutenant-generals from their jobs. Now, so Eisenhower gave Devers a task which the Supreme Commander thought even he, with his limited capacity for command, could probably carry out.

Devers' Seventh Army, commanded by General Patch, would advance north from its present position on the Rhine and fill in the gaps left in Lorraine and the German Saar by the departure of Patton's Third Army. Under other circumstances Eisenhower would have dearly loved to have ordered Seventh Army into action with Patton's Third. Patch's eight or so divisions were badly needed in the Ardennes. But there was a catch. Due to what Eisenhower thought was a lack of effort on Devers' part, his other army, the French First, had been unable to clear a sizeable force of German troops from French soil. One month earlier General Wiese's German 19th Army had stubbornly dug themselves in on the *western* bank of the Rhine around the French town of Colmar. Now the French were basically employed in containing this 'Colmar Pocket' and could not be used to fill in the gap that would have been left if the Seventh Army were used offensively. So Eisenhower was forced to tie the Seventh up in a strictly defensive operation. Just before he left, he gave Devers strict instructions what he was to do if his command were attacked by other German forces not so far accounted for by Allied Intelligence. If these 'missing' German divisions struck his command, he was to give ground 'slowly on his northern flank, even if he had to move completely back to the Vosges'. He was not allowed to let the 'Germans re-enter those mountains and this line was definitely laid down as the one that must be held on Devers' front'.⁹ The Supreme Commander did not want another Ardennes debacle.

Thus, as Eisenhower roared away in his armoured car, surrounded by heavily armed outriders (it was reported that German paras had been dropped behind Allied lines to kill the Supreme Commander), the big, bald General, whose grandmother had been born within fifty miles of where he was now standing, was left to ponder his new assignment. His Seventh Army would now have to take over a front eighty miles long, which had once been held by *two* armies. Not only that, he was faced with the presence of nearly one hundred thousand troops on *his* side of the Rhine, locked up, for the time being at least, in the Colmar Pocket! And if he was attacked, he was to put up only a token defence, giving up ground which had been paid for in American blood.

We do not know General Devers' mood that day. Alone of the senior American generals, he has still not found a biographer. But as he waited for his staff car in the cobbled yard of the Maginot Caserne he must have realized just how little faith Eisenhower had in him. For the first time in the six-month-long campaign in Western Europe, the Supreme Commander had specifically ordered one of his generals, if trouble came, to withdraw. The army which prided itself that it *never* gave up ground it had 'bought with its own blood' was now going to do so, and he, Jacob Devers, would command that withdrawal.

In the last years of the Second World War, any observant visitor to one of the major US headquarters in Europe might well have spotted them – a truck, a handful of tents, perhaps a van bristling with aerials, discreetly tucked in an orchard or behind a barn, and all manned by men wearing the blue uniform of the Royal Air Force.

'What,' the observant visitor might well ask, 'were RAF men, and mostly of low rank, doing at a higher headquarters, where full colonels were a dime a dozen?' These 'secret limeys', as they were called, were in fact members of the Special Liaison Unit (SLU), set up by the British Secret Service earlier in the war to maintain and guard the most precious secret of them all, what Winston Churchill called his 'very reliable sources'. This was the secret information provided by British Intelligence's own highly skilled decoding branch, the Code and

Cipher School, mockingly called by its members 'the Golf Club and Chess Society'. At the school, based at Bletchley in Buckinghamshire, the staff could decipher top-secret German orders and messages sent by their Enigma coding machine almost as quickly as the German recipients. But 'C', as the head of the Secret Service was called, knew that the only way to maintain the security of this amazing intelligence coup was to limit the knowledge of the Bletchley operation to as few people as possible, and this was where the SLUs came in. Attached to top-level battle headquarters, the SLUs received 'Ultra' (as the high-level decodes were called) by means of a one-time pad and later by the Typex machine, a ciphering system similar to Enigma. The Ultra information would be taken personally by the officer in charge of the SLU to the commanding general or his deputy. The latter would be allowed to read and digest the message, but the actual message form would have to be handed back to the SLU officer for destruction. Thus did the Allied commanders know what the Germans were going to do.

During the campaign in Europe in 1944/45 Ultra intelligence had served the Allies well on half-a-dozen major occasions. In August, 1944, for example, Ultra had warned that Hitler had ordered a four-division armoured strike against General Hodges' 1st US Army at Mortain. Hodges, forewarned, had soon put a stop to the German attempt to cut through to the coast and isolate Patton's Third Army in Brittany.

And so it had gone on throughout the Allied advance across France, Belgium and Holland towards the German frontier. But as the Germans fell back a change had begun to take place. The *Wehrmacht* had started to use the Reich's safe network of telephones and teleprinters which Bletchley could not tap. Top-level intelligence had virtually dried up.

That had been the situation throughout November and into December, 1944. Then at one minute after midnight on Saturday, 16 December the night shift at Bletchley was alerted. For weeks, with no messages of any importance coming from Germany, the staff in the cryptanalytical and processing huts had begun to believe that the war had passed them by.* They were jaded, too, by the months of concentrated effort since D-Day. Now, suddenly, the German High Command, after long weeks of absolute silence, was transmitting again. Tensely the staff waited for the first Enigma message to be

---

* For those interested in such things, the huts are still there.

decoded. It was from no less a person than Field-Marshal Gerd von Rundstedt himself and it was addressed to his field commanders. It read: 'The hour of destiny has struck. Mighty offensive armies face the Allies. Everything is at stake. More than mortal deeds are required as a holy duty to the Fatherland.'[10] The Battle of the Bulge had begun.

That Saturday even the SLU men in Europe were caught by surprise. One of them, John Weston, attached to General Bradley's head-quarters in Luxembourg, recalled over forty years later how on the afternoon of that Saturday 'I was in the little village of Echternach on the Luxembourg/German border. German spotter planes were in evidence. That same night Rundstedt's forces attacked. To say there was some confusion was to understate the position. Due to the radio blackout ordered by Hitler . . . there was very little Ultra intelligence. Hence the surprise.'[11]

But now back in Bletchley, the boffins were working all out, listening to the whole German front, almost five hundred miles of it, trying to discover where those 'missing' German divisions were located and how they might be employed. And one of the areas which came under their scrutiny was Alsace-Lorraine, held by the armies of General Jacob Devers.

Heavily wooded and very rugged for the most part, save for the Rhine plain and the area which borders on the German Saar, Alsace-Lorraine had been fought over for centuries. Originally neither French nor German, it had been snatched back and forth by the heirs of Charlemagne's great Frankish Empire until, in 1648, Louis XIV made it part of France. Over two centuries later, in 1870, Germany annexed most of Alsace and part of Lorraine by force and made Alsace-Lorraine a *Reichsland*, an Imperial territory, governed by German officials, virtually under the same terms as their new African colonies. For nearly fifty years the area was German, its menfolk conscripted into the German Army, its official language German, with French forbidden by law, until, in 1918, the French regained their lost provinces, again by force.

In 1940 Alsace-Lorraine changed hands once more. After the fall of France Alsace and part of Lorraine were reincorporated into the German Reich, their citizens becoming *Reichsdeutsche*. Not only that. In order to encourage the process of 'Germanization', this time the German authorities resettled thousands of ethnic Germans in the area, giving them land and encouraging them to marry the 'natives'. Naturally, Alsatians were drafted into the *Wehrmacht* and mostly sent off to fight on the Eastern Front where there would be little danger of them deserting to the enemy. Many, too, believing in the Nazi cause, volunteered for the German Army, and not only for the *Wehrmacht*. Some were even prepared to volunteer for the *Waffen SS*. Indeed, one-third of the elite 2nd SS Panzer Division '*Das Reich*' now advancing towards Bastogne was made up of Alsatians! Virtually everyone in that French border province had a relative serving in the German Army.

It was not surprising, therefore, that German Intelligence was well aware of what was now going on in the area, as Patton's men moved from the Saar to fight in the Bulge and Devers' soldiers moved northwards to fill the gap. They had their agents and sympathizers in every village and hamlet. Any of those simple farmers, who amused the GIs with their enormous meals of sauerkraut, laden with pork chops, sausages, and fat-belly pork, or horrified them by the way they hand-stuffed grain down the necks of their geese to produce the world-famed *paté de foie gras*, might well be an informer. There was a constant flow of information about American troop movements and formations across the Rhine as Christmas Eve approached and Patton's offensive got underway.

SS Colonel Linger, commander of the 17th SS Panzer Grenadier Division, who was later captured in Alsace, told his interrogators: 'When the breakthrough in the Ardennes had been stopped by the Allies, it was realized that several American divisions had been sent north to aid the Americans in their defence. It was therefore decided to launch an attack against what we felt sure to be a weak position.'[12]

Indeed German information was so good about the movements and dispositions of the *Amis*, as they called the Americans, on the other side of the Rhine that one day *before* Patton began his attack into the Bulge on 22 December, German Army Group G was ordered to exploit the situation in Alsace-Lorraine. On that day Hitler ordered German forces in the Saar to attack the Americans to gain the Saverne Gap in the Phalsbourg-Saverne sector in order to annihilate Devers' Seventh Army and to secure a juncture with the German Nineteenth Army in the Colmar Pocket.

For this purpose two assualt groups were to be readied. The first was to attack from east of the Blies River towards the south. Here it would breach the Maginot Line at Rohrbach and line up with the right flank of the second group for an attack on Phalsbourg. The second group was to attack from east of the fortress town of Bitche towards the south in several spearheads. After linking up with the first group, both were to attack towards the Phalsbourg-Saverne line.

Forty-eight hours after the attack in the north, shocktroops from Army Group Upper Rhine on the eastern bank of the river would attack across it. Their aim would be to establish bridgeheads to north and south of Strasbourg. In the meantime Wiese's Nineteenth Army would break out of the Colmar Pocket in two prongs. One would drive for Saarebourg to link up with the forces coming down from the north. The other would cut through the French First Army and head for Strasbourg, where it would join up with the shocktroops coming from the Rhine bridgeheads.

If the attack succeeded, the German High Command reasoned, it would provide a highly needed shot in the arm for the war-weary German people. The re-capture of Strasbourg, which held a special place in German hearts, just as it did in French ones, would be a tremendous propaganda coup, one which the 'Poison Dwarf'* in Berlin would make the most of. A German victory would also have very valuable military and political results. The destruction of Devers' Seventh Army would certainly bring all American offensive action in the Ardennes to a halt. More importantly, if Strasbourg and the Alsace were recaptured, their loss would certainly bring down General de Gaulle's shaky provisional government in Paris. The communist *resistance*, numbering millions and probably still armed, in spite of de Gaulle's efforts to disarm them, would definitely try to seize power and Allied communications and supply lines through France would be thrown into complete disarray. Perhaps, with luck, the whole Allied coalition in the West would collapse.

This, then, was the plan, and the Führer himself had set the time and date for this new surprise attack, the last of the war in the West. Operation Northwind would begin at twenty-three hundred hours on 31 December, 1944. Adolf Hitler was going to give Devers' young soldiers in the freezing hills and remote hamlets of Alsace-Lorraine a New Year's Eve surprise they would not forget.

A week before the start of Operation Northwind Devers had completed his take-over of Patton's old positions. His Seventh Army now occupied an eighty-four-mile front from the Rhine to a point a few miles west of Saarbrucken, and a flank along the Rhine north and

---

* Minister of Propaganda, Dr Joseph Goebbels, so named on account of his small stature and vitriolic tongue.

south of Strasbourg. His VI Corps held positions on the right from the Rhine to Bitche, with the 79th and 45th Infantry Divisions in the line and the 14th Armored Division in reserve. On VI Corps' left flank, holding a front of ten miles with little more than a regiment, was Task Force Hudelson. On Task Force Hudelson's left flank XV Corps held the line running westwards to within a few miles of Saarbrucken, using the 100th, 44th and 103rd Infantry Divisions, with the 106th Cavalry Group on its left flank, keeping a very loose contact with Patton's Third Army. Along the Rhine itself, covering a front of forty miles, two task forces in regimental strength were deployed, elements of the 70th and 42nd Infantry Divisions, known again by the name of their commanders as Task Force Herren and Task Force Linden.

It was an enormous front to hold, even for veteran soldiers – the equivalent of six divisions, spread out over eighty-four miles and facing the best soldiers in Europe, perhaps in the world. But for the most part the young men of Devers' Seventh Army weren't even veterans. The men of his 42nd, 63rd and 70th Divisions had just arrived from the States and were as green as the growing corn. In the case of the 70th Infantry Division, its soldiers had still been training in Fort Leonard Wood two months before, men moving up into the front line as late as 27 December!

Others of Devers' Divisions, such as the 12th and 14th Armored and the 44th and 100th Divisions (the first two of which were being kept in reserve), had had limited combat experience in the December battles on the German border, but even they had been fleshed out with raw replacements straight from the 'repple depples'* to make up for their losses. In the whole of his long line Devers had only two really experienced divisions, the 79th Infantry (of which we will hear more later) and the veteran 45th Infantry Division, the 'Thunderbirds' (named after their divisional insignia).

The 'Thunderbirds' had first gone into action in Sicily in July, 1943, taking part in the first invasion of European territory. Before they set off for their first taste of combat, the then commander of the Seventh Army, General Patton, had regaled the green troops with one of his rough-tough fighting speeches, replete with the usual aggressive, blood-tingling obscenities: 'Battle is far less frightening than those who have never been in it are apt to think. . . . All this bullshit about thinking of your mother and your sweetheart . . . is emphasized by

---

* GI nickname for a replacement depot.

writers who describe battles not as they are but as writers who have never heard a hostile shot or missed a meal think they are. . . . Battle is the most magnificent competition in which a human being can indulge. . . . Remember in fist fights the attacker wins. . . . Attack ruthlessly, rapidly, viciously, and without rest. . . . Kill even civilians who have the stupidity to fight us.'[13]

Later, Patton said he thought his pep talk to the Forty-Fifth was 'a helluva good talk, one of my best.' It certainly had the desired effect on the green 'Thunderbirds'! Alexander Clifford, a British war correspondent, watched horrified as men of the 45th mowed down German PoWs with a heavy machine gun as they climbed out of a truck at Comiso Airfield. Clark Lee, an American correspondent, reported how a Sergeant Barry West, escorting thirty-six German PoWs back to the cage, stopped the column behind the front and shot the lot of them. A Captain Jerry Compton smoked out forty-three snipers and then lined them up against a barn and had them machine-gunned.

These incidents, when they came out, nearly cost Patton the command of the Third Army in the UK a year later, but by that time the Thunderbirds had been well and truly blooded in the bitter fighting that had followed in Italy. The landings in Southern France had been the 45th's next assignment and now, four months later, after the long hard slog through France from the Riviera, the veterans of the Thunderbird division were tired, old men before their time, best exemplified by the cartoons drawn by Sergeant Bill Mauldin who had been wounded while fighting with the 45th. Willy and Joe, tough, cynical, ill-disciplined and very worn, they were the real Thunderbirds this December.

Both Devers' reserve formations were veterans as well. The Third Infantry Division, 'the Rock of the Marne', as it called itself on account of its epic stand on the River Marne in 1918, was even more experienced than the 45th. It had first gone into action under Patton's command in North Africa in 1942. Thereafter it had fought in Sicily, at Anzio, had helped to capture Rome, and had taken part in the landings in Southern France. By the time the war would be finished it would have spent 531 days in combat, suffering over 30,000 casualties – more then any other US Division, gaining one fifth of all the Medals of Honor awarded to US Army troops in the Second World War, a record thirty-six.

The other reserve infantry division, the 36th (Texas) Division, had first gone into combat in September 1943 at the Salerno landings. The 36th saw heavy fighting at Salerno and San Pietro, but its real baptism of blood had been the assault crossing of the River Rapido a little later in the Italian campaign – a crossing which had ended in total disaster. Of the Division's 141st Regiment, which had gone into action three thousand strong, only forty men returned. In the end 1,681 men were posted dead, wounded or missing in the abortive Rapido attack. So heavy were the losses that after the war prominent Texans wanted an official enquiry into the conduct of General Mark Clark, the commander of the Fifth US Army, who had ordered the fatal attack. As one officer of the 36th told a correspondent bitterly, 'I had 184 men. . . . Forty-eight hours later, I had seventeen. If that's not mass murder, I don't know what is!'[14]

But the Division recovered from the Rapido disaster and went on to see much fighting in Italy and then in Southern France and on the drive to the German border. Now it, too, was tired and fleshed out with raw replacements. So when the German attack came, as the High Command knew it would come now, it would be left, in the main, to the new boys to do what had to be done in Alsace-Lorraine. For the weary veterans of the 3rd, 36th, and 45th, as the day of the German attack grew closer, the bold slogan of that dying year, 'Win the War by Forty-Four', had been replaced by a very cynical new one: 'Stay Alive in Forty-Five'.

On a clear but cold 26 December, 1944, while further north in the Ardennes Patton's Third Army was making its first tenuous contacts with the 'Battered Bastards of Bastogne', the Seventh Army was alerted for action. That day the G2 of the Seventh, Brigadier-General Eugene L. Harrison, received a warning of what was soon to come. It was an Ultra message from Bletchley via General Devers' headquarters. As the G2 noted in his diary at the time, not giving any indication of how the vital information had been obtained: 'Excellent enemy sources indicate enemy units building up in Black Forest area* for offensive. Other indications for enemy action exist. Imperative that all defensive precautions be immediately effective.'[15]

That day both Devers and General Alexander Patch, commanding the Seventh Army, shifted their headquarters far to the rear. Neither of them wanted to suffer the fate of General Hodges, commanding the US 1st Army, who had had to flee from his headquarters at Spa in the Ardennes when it had seemed about to be overwhelmed.

---

* The German Black Forest just across the Rhine from the Seventh Army's positions.

That same day Devers went to see Eisenhower at his HQ in the Petit Trianon outside Paris. He explained that all his Intelligence sources indicated that he was soon going to be attacked in the Alsace-Lorraine area. Perhaps Devers hoped for additional units to bolster up his dangerously thin line. But there were no reserves. They were all committed in the Ardennes. Or perhaps he thought that Eisenhower might change his orders and give his armies a more aggressive role in the coming battle. We do not know. All we know from the Supreme Commander himself is that he repeated his orders of the 19th: 'I told Devers he must on no account permit sizeable formations to be cut off and surrounded.'[16]. The implication was clear. When the attack came, Devers was to put up token resistance and then retreat into the High Vosges mountains, surrendering the lowlands to the Germans; and if he did that, *then Strasbourg would fall into German hands for the third time in the last seventy-odd years!* A major political crisis was beginning to brew.

Tension was beginning to mount in the huge area covered by Devers' command. Parallel with the great scare in the Ardennes, caused by the appearance of Skorzeny's commandos and the scattered drop of Colonel von der Heydte's paras in the Belgian High Venn country, now reports of German paras landing behind Seventh and First Armies' lines came flooding in from all sides. They were reported dropping behind the front in the wooded Niederbronn area. Others were said to be landing at Phalsbourg, which until recently had been General Patch's HQ. Others were seen floating down near the Saverne Gap.

Captain Donald Pence, a new boy from the 70th Infantry, recalled later how his men sighted enemy patrols everywhere (though there weren't any) and how they worried about the 'Krauts just over the hill' from their positions, getting 'loaded up on Schnapps for their next attack'.

General de Lattre, the autocratic commander of the First French Army, known behind his back as 'King Jean', was alerted by Devers' HQ that 'parachute commandos have been dropped at various points in the rear of the Western Front'.[17] He was advised to put the men guarding his lines of communication on red alert, for 6th Army Group thought these German commandos were attempting to cut his communications through the vital Belfort Gap below the Colmar Pocket.

Hastily, de Gaulle in Paris mobilized whatever reserves he could find to protect the rear areas of the front. As far back as Lille, not far from the Channel coast, and Nancy, still officially Patton's HQ, officers in command were ordered 'to hold themselves ready to carry out without delay and with all resources at their disposal any especially urgent tasks requested by the Allied authorities,' whatever might be the state of the equipment of their troops.[18]

In fact, their equipment was virtually non-existent. The formations in the rear line areas were a rag-and-bobtail lot. The ones being hastily mobilized in Lille, for instance, had either a battledress blouse or an overcoat, but never both. Others were clad and armed with the military cast-offs of four Armies, the American, British, Canadian – *and German.* In other instances General Dody, the overall land commander, noted that some units were 'still in civilian clothes and had merely sky-blue overcoats unrecognized by the Allies'.[19]

In the end the French High Command managed to scrape together some fifty thousand men for rear line duty, guarding crossroads, railway installations, and the like, though General Dody thought them 'not fit to fight'. One division, the Tenth Infantry, was to be sent into the line around the Colmar Pocket; but the Tenth's sole contribution to what was to come was not exactly calculated to enhance Franco-American relations. On the way up to the new front its troop train stopped at Amagré-Lucqy station, not far from the city of Laon. There, one regiment of the Tenth systematically looted a stationary train full of Christmas presents from 'back home' intended for American troops in the line. The theft was immediately hushed up, but it caused quite a stir at the time.

On the same day that the Tenth was alerted for action, all the commanding generals of German Army Group G were taken from the Army Group HQ at Wachenheim to Hitler's own battle headquarters for the Battle of the Bulge at Ziegenberg Castle, not far from Giessen. Here they were searched, their briefcases examined and their pistols taken away from them, as was customary since the attempt to assassinate the Führer the previous July. Hitler no longer trusted the men who, in the good days, had achieved such victories for him. Then they were ushered into the presence of the Führer and Gerd von Rundstedt. After the usual preliminaries Hitler began to speak, and for the first time many of those present realized that their mostly battered and sadly depleted units, which had suffered grievously in the month-long frontier battles, were now being committed to a new surprise counterattack in Alsace-Lorraine. But, for once, the Führer seemed almost reasonable. He told them, 'The task set for this new offensive does not go beyond what is possible and can be achieved with our available forces. We are committing eight divisions. With the exception of one division which comes from Finland, seven are, of course, worn out from fighting. . . . But the enemy opposing us – if we have luck with five divisions, possibly only four or even three – is not fresh either. . . . We shall find a situation which we could not wish to better. . . . If this operation succeeds it will lead to the destruction of a part of that group of divisions which confronts us south of the breakthrough point. The next operation will then follow immediately. It will be connected with a further push. I hope that in this way we shall first smash these American units in the South. Then we shall continue the attack and shall try to connect it with the real long-term operation itself. . . . This second attack has an entirely clear objective – the destruction of the enemy forces. No questions of prestige are involved. It is not a question of gaining space. The exclusive aim is to destroy and eliminate the enemy forces wherever we find them. It is not even the task of this operation to liberate all Alsace. That would be wonderful. It would have an immense effect on the German people, a decisive effect on the world, immense psychological importance, a very depressing effect on the French people. But that is not what matters. As I said before, *what matters is the destruction of the manpower of the enemy*. . . . I consider it a particularly good omen that in German history New Year's night has always been of good military omen. The enemy will consider New Year's night an unpleasant disturbance because he does not celebrate Christmas but New Year. . . . When, on New Year's Day, the news spreads in Germany that the German offensive has been resumed at a new spot and that it is meeting with success, the German people will conclude that the old year was miserable at the end but that the new year has a good beginning. That will be a good omen for the future. *Meine Herren*, I want to wish each of you, individually, good luck!'[20]

As New Year's Eve approached, the tension mounted. In the 100th Infantry, the 'Century Division', Intelligence reported that US PoWs were being asked by their German captors about their gas masks and the state of gas training in the US Army. Immediately the alarm went out. The Germans were going to use gas. At once the Division started to re-issue gas masks to their troops who had long flung them away.

On 28 December another alert was sounded. It was reported that many German sympathizers who had fled with the retreating Germans the previous November were coming back. There was going to be a mass drop of French saboteurs throughout Alsace-Lorraine. All foreigners wandering about rural Alsace were ordered to be rounded up. Most of these, supposedly Poles working on the land, were now declared to be German agents, who would provide 'safe houses' for the French saboteurs soon to be parachuted into the rural areas.

The next day, Devers, at 6th Army Group, radioed Patch: 'A hostile attack against your flank west of Bitche may force you to give up ground from your main position. To meet such a possibility it is necessary that your west flank be protected by a reserve battle position. With this in mind, reconnaissance and organization of a reserve battle position will be instituted without delay. . . . One half of each division and attached troops currently earmarked as SHAEF reserve located in your area may be employed at any given period to assist in organization of ground, provided troops so employed can be reassembled and prepared for movement on eight-hour notice'.[21]

Even before the battle had begun, it was clear that Devers had accepted the inevitable – he'd run first and then, perhaps, he'd live to fight again.

On the night of 30 December small-arms fire was reported at a dozen different spots along the American front. Was it just the usual 'nervous nellies' firing at shadows, or was it someone firing at Germans attempting to probe the American forward positions? Who was firing at whom? No one knew.

At the hamlet of Lichtenberg an American officer appeared and ordered that the village concert scheduled for New Year's Eve should be stopped. Why? What did he know, the puzzled, apprehensive villagers asked themselves. In Wingen, as they celebrated morning Mass, fireworks stored for the New Year's celebration* (or so they said) exploded and blew up part of the main road nearby. Later, people would say, it had been the Germans who had done it. After all, Wingen was going to become a key spot in the battle to come. At the border village of Althausen, some small boys who had skipped Mass said later that they had seen a German patrol coming in out of the hills. That morning, as the first heavy snowfall of the winter began to fall, refugees, their carts piled with their bits and pieces, began to

* Fireworks are used to celebrate the Alsatian New Year.

trudge out of the hamlet of Heideneck, heading for La Petite-Pierre, although not a single shot had yet been fired. Among them were the priest and the mayor, the two officials most likely to be arrested when the Gestapo returned. What did they know? What had they heard? The 'Prussians', as they still called the Germans in their local dialect, had come this way in 1870 and 1940. Was it just instinct or was it something else that had told them the Prussians were coming again? Behind them they left the old and those too sick to flee, *and those who would welcome the returning Prussians!*

On New Year's Eve the man whose army was going to bear the brunt of the attack to come, General Alexander Patch, commander of the US Seventh Army, visited his two corps commanders, General Brooks of VI Corps and General Haislip of XV Corps, at the latter's command post at the village of Fénétrange.

Patch, a tall balding man whose face was marked by deep lines etched from his nose to the corners of his mouth, had seen much of war in France. In 1917 he had commanded a machine-gun battalion working with the French. In the Second World War he had commanded a corps at Guadalcanal so successfully that he had been given command of the US Seventh Army which had fought all the way from the beaches to the Reich. Now he knew that he was about to wage his third battle on French soil. For Ultra and his Intelligence men knew the German attack was imminent. Eight thousand reinforcements, they had discovered, had been ferried across the Rhine to Wiese's Nineteenth Army in the Colmar Pocket. Reinforcements, they had learned, were being hastily shipped to the 17th SS Panzer Grenadier Division, currently facing Brooks' Sixth Corps. The German 21st Panzer Division was moving south along the Rhine – indication after indication, and they all mounted up to one thing. As General Patch told his two commanders bluntly, Brooks and Haislip could expect an all-out attack on their fronts in the early hours of New Year's Day.

It was the last day of 1944. In the heady days of non-stop victory back in the autumn, many of the Top Brass, Montgomery and Eisenhower among them, had thought that the Second World War in Europe would be over by now. Instead the Germans were still attacking furiously in the Ardennes and the worried generals sitting around the rough wooden table in that remote village knew that it would soon be their turn. The actors were in place, the stage was set, the drama could begin.

PART I

Attack!

'The world must know that this State, will, therefore, never capitulate!

Adolf Hitler, 1 January, 1945

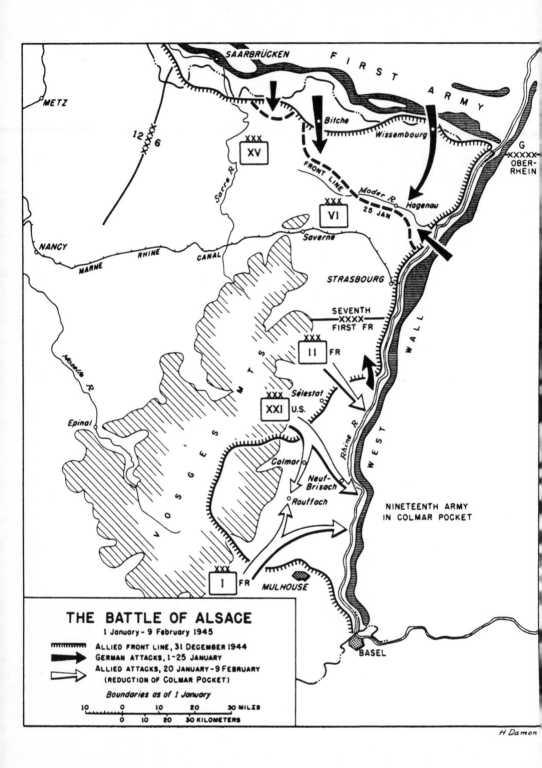

METZ

SAARBRÜCKEN

FIRST ARMY

12 XXXX 6

XXX
XV

Bitche

Wissembourg

Sarre R.

G
XXXXX
OBER-
RHEIN

FRONT LINE

Moder R. 25 JAN

Hogenau

XXX
VI

NANCY

RHINE

MARNE

CANAL

Saverne

STRASBOURG

Moselle R.

VOSGES MTS

SEVENTH
XXXX
FIRST FR

XXX
II FR

Epinal

XXX
XXI U.S.

Sélestat

Rhine R.

WEST WALL

Colmar

Neuf-
Brisach

Rouffach

NINETEENTH ARMY
IN COLMAR POCKET

XXX
I FR

MULHOUSE

BASEL

THE BATTLE OF ALSACE
1 January - 9 February 1945

▬▶ ALLIED FRONT LINE, 31 DECEMBER 1944
➡ GERMAN ATTACKS, 1-25 JANUARY
⇨ ALLIED ATTACKS, 20 JANUARY-9 FEBRUARY
(REDUCTION OF COLMAR POCKET)

Boundaries as of 1 January

10   0   10   20   30 MILES
0   10   20   30 KILOMETERS

H Damon

ONE

Just before midnight on the last day of the old year, Sunday, 31 December, 1944, two young officers, Lieutenant George Bradshaw and Lieutenant Richard Shattuck, decided that someone ought to celebrate the advent of 1945 in the 44th Infantry Division's Fox Company. In spite of the freezing cold the two officers were in high spirits as they clambered out of their snowbound foxholes to wait for midnight.

For nearly two days now the relatively green 44th Infantry had been dug in between the industrial towns of Sarreguemines and Rimling along the River Blies at the extreme left of the Seventh Army's long line. In spite of the current alert and the tension which had been rising steadily ever since Christmas, the Division had experienced little save minor skirmishes and artillery duels. Although the men in the line had not been told officially that there was a 'flap' on, they knew from their contacts with local civilians and the anxious looks on the faces of visiting staff officers that soon, as they phrased it in their crude slang 'the shit was gonna hit the fan'. Why should they have to stand to virtually every night, with double the normal number of men in the line, if the Top Brass were not expecting some kind of an attack?

On the night of 30 December, it had appeared that trouble was coming their way. In the small hours the infantrymen had been startled by the sound of a booby trap going off. It had been followed by another, and another. In all five of the carefully-laid warnings traps to their front had exploded. All night they had tensed over their weapons, hardly daring to breathe, fancying every new shadow was a German crawling into the attack. But it had been a false alarm after all.

The five boobys had been set off by two rabbits, whose dead bodies were added to the usual cans of hash to make a splendid New Year's breakfast of 'S and S', otherwise known more crudely as 'shit on shingle'. *

Now, unabashed by the fact that the Germans were going to attack at any moment, the two young lieutenants stood in the moonlit snow, carbines raised to fire a *feu de joie* on the stroke of midnight, while in the freezing foxholes the dogfaces grinned at the crazy antics of the two high-spirited officers.

'Two minutes to go,' Bradshaw called to Shattuck. He clicked off his safety catch and prepared to fire, as he started to count off the seconds to 1945.

But Bradshaw was not fated to fire his salute to 1945. Suddenly machine-gun bullets began kicking up the snow all around him. That same instant a fighter plane came zooming out of the moonlit sky, dragging its monstrous black shadow behind it across the snowfield, violent flame rippling the length of its wings, as it shot up Fox Company's positions. An instant later it had gone, roaring away in a tight curve. The two shaken officers rose to their feet, patting the snow from their uniforms.

'What the hell's going on, Dick?' Bradshaw called to his buddy.[1] Shattuck shook his head, but already he could hear the rattle of tank tracks to their front. Instinctively he knew this was it. The long-expected attack was coming in.

About the same time that the German fighter shot up the positions of the 44th's 114th Regiment, Sergeant Luther Ott of its sister regiment, the 71st Infantry Regiment, holding the line from Bliesbruck eastward to Rimling, was trudging through the snow on patrol. Like the two high-spirited officers, his mind was half on the patrol and half on the New Year. He topped a small hill and suddenly all thoughts of New Year vanished. Later he recorded his astonishment at what he saw in the valley below: 'It was the biggest swarm of Krauts I'd ever seen in my life! They were all in white, moving in a kind of triangle formation, with the base of the triangle heading right for my company.'[2]

Sergeant Ott didn't hesitate, although he knew he was in danger of being overrun at any moment by the advancing Germans. He radioed to his CO, Captain Robert Sindenberg, what he had just seen, and then

* Hash on toast.

ran back with the rest of the patrol through the deep snow, as the men of the XIII SS Corps began their attack.

In Berlin, Hitler began to shout shrilly into the microphones of the 'Poison Dwarf's' radio network: 'Our people are resolved to fight the war to victory under any and all circumstances. . . . We are going to destroy everybody who does not take part in the common effort for the country or who makes himself a tool of the enemy. . . . The world must know that this State will, therefore, never capitulate. . . . Germany will rise like a phoenix from its ruined cities and this will go down in history as the miracle of the 20th Century!

'I want, therefore, in this hour, as spokesman of Greater Germany, to promise solemnly to the Almighty that we shall fulfil our duty faithfully and unshakeably in the New Year, in the firm belief that the hour will strike when victory will ultimately come to him who is most worthy of it, the Greater German Reich.'[3]

The last German counterattack of the Second World War in the West – Operation Northwind – had begun.

By one o'clock that Monday morning the whole divisional front of the 44th Infantry Division was being engaged by the enemy. On the Division's left flank the 114th Infantry Regiment beat off a determined effort by the Germans to exploit a bridgehead across the River Blies. A massive artillery bombardment was brought down upon the white-clad attackers and they reeled back, pinned down on the west bank of the Blies.

In the centre the threat to the 324th was more intense. Three times the German attackers tried to cross the River Blies and three times they were thrown back. But the most serious threat to the 44th Infantry came on the left flank, held by the 71st Infantry Regiment. There the Germans attacked in strength, crying, as they ran into the assault, 'Die Yankee bastard!' or 'Come and fight Yankee gangsters', almost as if they were under the influence of booze or drugs.

Here the German thrust could not be stopped. A German five-company assault north of Rimling curled round the right flank of the 71st's First Battalion and forced it to withdraw 1000 yards. The Regiment's Third Battalion was whistled up to restore the lost position. To no avail. Already over 600 Germans had penetrated the First's positions and occupied the forest to their rear, 2000 yards further on. In the confused night fighting, the Third was diverted for an assault on the forest. They did not get far. In the thick clumps of trees, knee deep in snow, companies soon broke into disorganized platoons and sections, as the fight developed into a confused mix-up. A reserve battalion of the 324th was thrown in to help, but the heavily outnumbered Germans held on stubbornly. The month-long battles along the well-wooded frontiers of the Reich had made them veterans in this kind of fighting; and as always the German NCOs who commanded the small isolated sections were flexible, quick to react, and masters of using a single machine gun to cover firebreaks and trails, so that a handful of defenders might well hold up a whole company of attackers.

In the end the two battalions gave up. They sealed off the southern edge of the forest and dug in. The 2nd Battalion fared little better. Aided by a platoon of Shermans it regained its original positions by six that morning, only to be thrown out again by a German counterattack one hour later. Now the 44th Infantry Division's link with its right-hand neighbour, the 100th Division, was beginning to crumble. But that was not the only problem facing the 'Century' men as dawn broke. To their right the paper-thin line of Task Force Hudelson was under severe attack by elements of two German divisions. In essence, the 100th Division stood a definite risk of being cut off, the very fate about which Eisenhower had warned Devers only days before.

Task Force Hudelson, consisting of the 62nd Armored Infantry Battalion, the 117th Cavalry Reconnaissance Squadron, some combat engineers, mortar crews, a tank destroyer outfit, and the 94th Cavalry, had been preparing their link-up position some ten miles long between the 100th and 45th Divisions for nearly two weeks now. They had worked hard to dig in their machine guns, set trip-flares, sow minefields, so as to make the most of their few numbers. All the same their positions were at least twenty yards apart and in the darkness their commander knew the Germans could feed in whole platoons between his widely spread foxholes without the defenders even noticing. He knew, too, that this position would be an ideal target for the attackers. Indeed so much importance was given to penetrating the Hudelson line by the Germans that a special code-name had been adopted for the attack: '*Tenth May, 1940*', a date of great significance for the *Wehrmacht*. For on that day, five years before, the victorious German assault on the West had begun.

That morning when the enemy hit the Task Force, its main

component, the 62nd Armored Infantry Battalion, was waiting to be relieved by the 70th Infantry Division.

'Sure hate to be relieved in this quiet sector,' Captain Trammell of the 62nd told Captain Long of the 70th's advance party. But there would be no relief for the unsuspecting 62nd this dawn. When Task Force Hudelson finally left the line it would be a beaten, decimated formation. Soon after midnight, elements of two whole German divisions, the 256th and the 361st Volksgrenadier Divisions, started to probe the Task Force's positions along their entire front. First struck was the 94th Cavalry Reconnaissance Squadron in the centre, which was soon broken. All that the helpless soldiers could do was to form small groups and, as the Divisional History puts it euphemistically, 'effect an escape by flight'.

At five-thirty the Germans attacked in strength. Without the warning of a preliminary barrage, they rushed the Task Force line. To the surprised defenders there seemed to be hundreds of them, streaming suddenly out of the woods in white camouflage suits. Some tried the old tricks on the Americans. '*Hold your fire!*' they yelled and the Americans did just that, thinking the Germans were coming in to surrender.

Rapidly the American line began to break down. Captain Trammell, who had so hated to leave this 'quiet sector', called back to his commander, Colonel Myers, 'My men are being cut to pieces!'

But there was nothing Myers could do about it. The Task Force's front was being swamped everywhere. On the left flank the 117th Cavalry Reconnaisance Squadron had been virtually surrounded at Mouterhouse. The 62nd was fighting for its life, withdrawing through the village of Bannstein down the road which led to Philippsbourg. The 94th Cavalry Reconnaissance Squadron had disappeared.

In Bannstein everyone – cooks and clerks included – pitched in in an attempt to stop the victorious Volksgrenadiers. Sergeant Borjourguez manned a mortar on his own and held off thirty Germans trying to outflank the place. Even when he was wounded in the foot he refused to be evacuated. But there was no stopping them. The men of the 62nd began to break up into small groups in order to escape, leaving behind their vehicles. One group under Sergeant Hargett ran into the enemy and, although the sergeant was shot in both arms, he managed to get through.

Ammunition began to run out. The supporting artillery came under direct enemy small arms fire. Germans were sniping at their positions from less than fifty yards away. The end at Bannstein was close.

Captain Long, of the 275th Infantry Regiment's advance party coming up to relieve the 62nd, was billeted in their Bannstein CP that morning. Long and two companions, who had never heard a shot fired in anger, were too excited at the prospect of action to be scared as they set off up the road to witness the battle. Moving out at 'a smart trot', as Long recalled years later, they were 'met almost immediately by a mass of American soldiers in full retreat. We saw the hopelessness of the situation and turned back to the large, two-storey CP. The whole countryside was aflame and it was almost like daylight from the burning barns, small houses, fences etc.'[4] Young Captain Long realized that war was not exactly what he supposed it to have been from the lectures at Fort Leonard Wood.

By eleven o'clock Bannstein was completely cut off. Those who could still walk had already abandoned any hope of getting out of the trap by vehicle. These they abandoned and were plodding up the steep snowbound hills making for the next village of Baerenthal. Behind them they left their wounded and their dead. Triumphantly their white-clad attackers swarmed into the village.

Lieutenant-Colonel Hudelson had almost run out of reserves. He had thrown in all his available infantry and they had still not been able to stop the Germans. He appealed to the only outfit not yet committed, the 125th Engineers. Its A Company was ordered into action south of Bannstein. Captain Robert Knight, their CO, told his officers, 'Here's the deal. We're spread mighty thin. That's why we're being used for infantry.' Swiftly he allotted his platoon commanders their tasks, ending with the warning, 'Move quickly!'[5]

But it was already too late. As the engineers moved up through the snow, they could see abandoned equipment – and bodies – every-where. As they passed the double-apron barbed-wire fence they had put up two days before, they found it 'hanging with dead and dying Germans. Some were hanging limply, some moved, and some lay and screamed. They were covered with a light coat of new fallen snow.'[6]

Sergeant William Godfrey's squad was ambushed almost at once. He had just muttered 'One hell of a way to start off the New Year!' as his half-track ground its way up an icy hill when there was a flash of scarlet. Close by an enemy burp gun ripped off a volley. Godfrey was slammed against the side of the cab by a sledge-hammer blow. Slowly the half-track began to fall over.

Godfrey regained consciousness to find himself stripped naked, save for his pants, by the Germans, his legs trapped beneath the five-ton half-track. Around him there were four members of his squad, all dead and stripped naked. Next to him there was a naked GI, with a bullet hole right between his eyes. Further up the road he could hear German soldiers talking and the sound of digging.

Freezing and in terrible pain from his wound, he found his trench knife and started digging his legs free. He dug until he was bathed in sweat and there were blisters on his hands. But he managed it. Somehow or other he struggled back to his own lines.

Inevitably the Engineers' attack failed. They could do little against German armour and artillery. In the end they too pulled back in their remaining vehicles. Nearly a third of the company had vanished and many more had been wounded.

Hudelson threw in his precious last reserve, the 19th Armored Infantry Battalion. Its orders were to stop the Germans at all costs. The men didn't get far. As what was left of the cavalry reconnaissance outfits pulled back through them in something akin to panic, they were stuck by an all-out attack as the Germans followed close on the heels of the retreating cavalrymen. The officers knew they didn't stand a chance if they decided to fight. They would be encircled and overrun. Hastily the order was given for them to withdraw. Some of the infantrymen didn't like the idea of withdrawal one bit. Mortar Sergeant Schickel, still game for a fight in spite of the chaos all around, yelled to his boss, Tech Sergeant Wright, 'Hey what's the target!'

Wright shouted back, 'Drop 'em in the wood. There are so many Krauts there you couldn't miss if you goddam tried!'[7]

Wright was right. There were enemy soldiers everywhere. Even the local civilians who were pro-German now joined in the attack on their 'liberators'. As the *Divisional History* of the 14th Armored Division records, one Frenchwoman who had up to now 'appeared friendly' to the Americans began sniping at the retreating GIs. She succeeded in killing one of them. Then, 'They (the GIs) cut her in half with a blast from quadruple 0.5 inch machine guns.'[8]

The survivors of Lieutenant-Colonel Hudelson's Task Force were now in full retreat. Everywhere there was chaos and confusion. Infantrymen, engineers, tankers, cavalrymen, gunners, all using the same narrow roads, skidding and sliding as the tracked vehicles slipped on the steep slopes. This was the big 'bug-out' and all of them knew it. The enemy was right behind them. As the *Divisional History* says: '(It was) like walking in a nightmare.'

Twenty-four hours before, listening to Colonel Hudelson briefing the new officers of the 70th Division in his Baerenthal CP, Captain Pence had had the 'distinct impression that, rather than expecting an attack, Hudelson was impatient at not being himself allowed to attack'.[9] Now his outfit was finished. By dusk on its first day of combat it would be stood down as a fighting force.

The task of trying to hold the area from Baerenthal to Dambach was now given to the 70th Infantry Division's 275th Regiment. It was a division that had never heard a shot fired in anger, led by senior officers whose last experience of combat had been in the First World War. A potential disaster seemed in the making.

For the veteran 45th Infantry Division the first day of 1945 dawned bright and beautiful. On their front, as yet, there was no sign of the great attack. As the Journal of the Division's 157th Infantry Regiment recorded: 'Jan. 1st 1945 was a clear cold day, the type of day Americans are apt to call perfect football weather.'[10] Back in the middle of December the morale of the Division had been badly affected by the first rumours from the Ardennes: 'The Normandy troops were fleeing back to the beaches'; 'Patton had been routed'; 'a tremendous new Dunkirk was in the making.' But morale had been restored by the good news now coming from Bastogne. So, as the first rumours started to spread in the divisional area about the plight of the 44th and the 100th Divisions, they did not take them too seriously.

But to their rear the 'feather merchants' and 'canteen commandos', as the service and supply troops were called contemptuously by the 'dogfaces', did. As the chronicler of the Division's 179th Regiment recalled afterwards: 'Rear echelons, remembering the fate of the 1st Army echelons, 7th Army HQ, 12 TAC HQ, huge trucking and ordnance outfits, all packed up and fled! Leaving food uneaten on the table, they "partied"* and never stopped until they had reached Luneville!'†

Traffic was paralysed. The roads were jammed with trucks, jeeps, trailers and vans, all going back. The terrible waste that always

* GI slang for 'left', from the French *partir*=to leave.
† New Seventh Army HQ.

follows an army was multiplied many times as equipment was abandoned. Like H. G. Wells' *The End of the World*, 'the rear pulled out as if the end had really come'.[11]

But now the 45th Division was drawn into the action. As the true position of Task Force Hudelson became clear, two battalions of the 179th Regiment were ordered up to fill the gap. It was a terrible march, with trucks slithering and sliding off the icy roads, past troops from the Rest Center fleeing westwards, past fleeing refugees, frightened old women and children, pulling carts piled with their worldly possessions, past columns of tanks of the 14th Armored Division 'moving in both directions at once,' as the chronicler of the 179th records, 'through a confusion that on a small scale must have resembled the French débâcle of '39'.[12]

Other units of the 45th Division now started to be drawn into the fight. The first probing attacks were against the 157th Regiment. Patrols began hitting their lines everywhere. A column of some 300 Germans with seventeen horse-drawn artillery pieces was spotted and an air attack was requested. In the perfect, clear weather it was thought the dive-bombers of the TAC airforce couldn't miss. But the 'American Luftwaffe', as it was often called due to the many times it had bombed its own troops (or 'Lootwaffe', from its habit of widespread looting) could, and it was only on the second attempt that the 'flyboys' were able to put the Germans to flight and the pressure on the 157th began to relax. But not for long. In the coming week the only veteran division that General Devers had in the line was to experience fighting just as tough as they had at Anzio the year before.

By now virtually all Devers' units were under attack by an estimated eight German divisions, and already by mid-afternoon on that Monday it was becoming clear that the 44th Infantry Division was the most endangered. On its left flank, in the vicinity of Gros Rederching, the Germans had forced elements of the 44th to withdraw, and by doing so they were, in turn, exposing the flank of the 100th Infantry Division. But there was worse to come. As the Division's 399th Infantry Regiment came under ever-increasing attack by the Germans, its S-3 was called by an unknown officer of the 117th Reconnaissance Squadron on their flank. 'We're falling back a little,' the cavalryman said lamely.

'How far is *a little?*' Major Convey, the S-3, snapped back.

'About two thousand yards.'

Convey knew what a withdrawal of that magnitude might do to the

Division's tactical position. 'Do you *have* to fall back that far?' he asked.[13]

His answer was a click on the phone. The unknown cavalryman had hung up. When next heard from, the 117th Cavalry had fallen back much more than two thousand yards. In fact, it had retreated *eight or nine* miles to south of the town of Wingen. There it found the enemy already in position and fled again. After that the 117th Cavalry disappeared from the combat zone completely. There would be work for the Inspector-General's branch once the battle was over.

The Germans now began to exploit the cavalry's flight and the 100th Division's wide open flank. They pressed home their attack, isolating and cutting off frightened groups of infantrymen. Some, however, were not so frightened. Instead of surrendering, as stragglers were beginning to do by the score, they dug in. One such group consisted of Pfcs Bower, Powell, Meza, Lane, McIntyre and Eyverson. They had been on outpost duty in a French school. Now they were surrounded by Germans, all exits blocked. They asked the French janitor, who had not fled with the rest, if there was any secret way out. He led them to a room where a window had recently been sealed up with cement blocks – 'galloping stones' as the locals called them. With their knives they began hacking away at the stones. Then they heard footsteps coming down the corridor. Andy Powell, a full-bloodied Red Indian, moved to the side of the door and waited. Just as the first stone came crashing to the floor a solid blow smashed the door panel. A German poked his head through, candle in hand. As the 100th Division's history recorded, 'That was a bad error and showed poor training. Powell blew the Kraut's stupid head off with one rifle shot!'[14]

Working feverishly, as more and more Germans flooded into the corridor, they enlarged the hole until they could clamber through. To their chagrin they found they were in another room. They ran through it. A German appeared but Meza was quicker on the draw. He cut him down with a burst from his tommy gun.

Alerted by the firing, Germans were now appearing everywhere. The Americans dashed down a corridor. Luck was with them. By accident they had stumbled into the basement furnace room, where they looked for a hiding place. All that afternoon they hid there, as the Germans combed the building. As night fell they decided to make a break for it down the corridor. To their horror they came across three weary Germans sleeping soundly in their path. Saying a prayer that they wouldn't wake up and the door beyond wouldn't squeak, they stepped over them one by one and sneaked outside. Half an hour later they reached the American lines to be challenged by a sentry with 'Halt! What's the password?'

As Bower said later, 'We could have kissed that sentry, beard and all!'[15]

TWO

The Supreme Commander had had a bad Monday. That morning the last major air strike by the *Luftwaffe* in the West had caught his air forces completely by surprise. Between six and ten o'clock over 1,000 German fighter-bombers had strafed, bombed and shot up virtually every Allied field in the Low Countries and Northern France. The German 'Operation Big Blow' had been a tremendous success. By the time it was over, twenty-seven Allied bases from Brussels to Eindhoven were in ruins and over 300 Allied aircraft had been knocked out. Even Montgomery's own personal Dakota had been wrecked.

Almost immediately Eisenhower ordered a cover-up. It was claimed that the attack had cost the Germans three hundred aircraft, though they had lost perhaps only a third of that number, and that it had had no effect on the Allied capacity for attack. In fact the Germans had succeeded in paralysing the Allied Tactical Air Force for more than a week. As French fighter-ace Pierre Clostermann wrote later: 'The American censorship and Press service, in a flat spin, tried to present this attack as a great Allied victory by publishing peculiar figures. We pilots were still laughing about them three months later!'[1]

Now Eisenhower was receiving further alarming news from Devers' Headquarters in Alsace. The Seventh Army's 44th Division had withdrawn slightly; the New York Rainbow Division, the 42nd, had done the same; while the 100th Division, both its flanks turned, had been forced to bend southwards to meet the threat from the east and what was, in effect, a second front at right angles to its original one.

Yet, in spite of the increasing German pressure on these green, untried divisions, Devers was *not* carrying out the orders Eisenhower had given him back in the last week of December. So far he had not even attempted to withdraw to one of the three fall-back lines they had agreed upon. In desperate need of fresh troops in the Ardennes – already he had been forced to use two and a half divisions of British troops to make up the gaps in the US Army – Eisenhower did not want to get heavily embroiled in Alsace-Lorraine. In addition, he guessed that the new attack had only been launched by Hitler to force him to withdraw troops from the Ardennes. There was only one strategy, he knew, for the Alsace-Lorraine sector, and that was withdrawal.

That afternoon Eisenhower told his fiery-tempered Chief-of-Staff, Bedell Smith – 'Somebody's got to be a sonovabitch about this headquarters!' – to tackle Devers about his tardiness in carrying out his orders. Devers had even asked for reinforcements! Eisenhower told Smith: 'You must call up Devers and tell him he is not doing what he was told, that is to get VI Corps back and to hold the Alsace Plain with recce and observational elements.'[2]

Eisenhower thought it would be possible to hold the area with light forces, for the attacking German divisions, he knew, were weak. Smith, the realist who knew how Ike dithered and changed his mind, didn't agree. Unlike Eisenhower, who saw things in grey, he visualized everything in black and white. He told his chief that Devers should either try to hold where he was or fall back completely. Smith wanted no second Ardennes, where divisions such as the US 106th Division had been cut off and forced to surrender back in mid-December.* But this time Eisenhower was adamant. 'The bulk of VI Corps *must* come back,' he snapped. 'But from this force mobile elements must be sent out to give warning of the enemy advance. The first principle when taking a defensive position is to reconnoitre as far as possible to your front.'[3] We do not know what Smith's reaction was to this lecture on elementary tactics, but loyally enough he started to carry out Eisenhower's instructions.

Curiously, Eisenhower, 'the political general', as he was generally regarded by orthodox military men in the Allied armies, seemed to have forgotten all the political considerations. If Devers *did* carry out this order, Strasbourg would be abandoned to the Germans and an estimated 150,000 citizens would be placed at risk. All those who had helped the Americans would be regarded as traitors by the German authorities. Technically, under German law, they were

---

* See C. Whiting, *Death of a Division*, for further details.

German citizens – *Reichsdeutsche* – and had been since 1940 when the Germans had declared Alsace part of the Third Reich.

But more was at stake than that. After Paris, Strasbourg ranked second in French hearts. Here Rouget de Lisle had composed 'La Marseillaise' in 1792. Here Alphonse Daudet had set his touching little story, *La Dernière Classe*, about a French schoolmaster's last lesson in the French language before the Prussian authorities imposed the German tongue on the children in 1871.*

How long would this symbol of French resurgence remain French? 'The Strasbourg question . . . was going to plague me throughout the Ardennes battle', wrote Eisenhower in his *Crusade in Europe*.

Up to now his plans for Alsace had remained a tight secret, known only to a handful of top-ranking US generals. As we have seen it had first been mentioned at the Verdun Conference on 19 December. Thereafter it had been ten days before the French became aware of what the Americans intended to do. On 27 December the French commander of the 1st French Army, General de Lattre, was summoned to Devers' HQ at Vittel and told that there was a possibility the Americans *might* be withdrawn in an emergency. One day later this was confirmed by Letter of Instruction Number Seven, which laid out the successive defensive positions the US Seventh Army would take in case of a German attack and envisaged a main American defence line along the eastern slopes of the Vosges Mountains.

On the same day General Juin, Chief of the French National Defence Staff, visited Eisenhower's Supreme Headquarters and learned of the Americans' intentions. But they were put to him as a purely hypothetical possibility, such as 'staffs are in the habit of considering, particularly in a defensive situation', as Juin wrote in his *Memoirs*. The General departed appeased, thinking it was all just a staff exercise. When he next appeared at SHAEF, the feathers would fly!

On 31 December de Lattre told General du Vigier, Military Governor of Strasbourg that 'the plan (outlined in Letter of Instruction Number Seven) was no more than a study of a certain hypothesis in which no one could believe under present circumstances'.[4]

This was the situation on 1 January when Juin reported to de Gaulle in Paris. Now the latter knew that the Americans had been attacked in Alsace. Neither Frenchman knew that at that very moment General

---

* Interestingly enough, as soon as the French took over again in 1918 and then again in 1944, they forbade German, which is the Alsatians' native tongue, and reimposed French. *Tout çà change . . .*

Devers had just arrived by air at Saverne from his headquarters in Vittel. With him he bore Bedell Smith's instructions to withdraw. Soon he would order General Patch, Commander of the Seventh Army, and General Brooks, Commander of the US VI Corps, to begin withdrawing the next day. By 5 January the three-stage withdrawal would have to be completed, meaning the abandonment of Northern Alsace and Strasbourg!

All the same de Gaulle, the prima donna ('Joan of Arc' Roosevelt called him contemptuously) sensed all was not well in Alsace. As he wrote afterwards, referring to himself in that strange oblique way, almost as if he were already dead and a historic figure, the abandonment of Alsace would be 'a terrible wound inflicted on the honor of our country and its soldiers, a terrible curse for the Alsatians to the despair of France, a profound blow to the nation's confidence in De Gaulle'.[5]

Accordingly the two first drafted a signal to de Lattre, telling him, 'Naturally the French Army cannot consent to the abandonment of Strasbourg. . . . In case the Allied forces retire from their present positions north of the French First Army lines, I order you to take matters into your own hands and to ensure the defense of Strasbourg.'[6]

Having ordered his senior officer at the front to be prepared to commit insubordination if necessary, de Gaulle wrote a letter to Eisenhower declaring that 'the French Government, for its part, obviously cannot let Strasbourg fall into enemy hands again without first doing everything possible to prevent it. . . . Whatever happens,' he concluded, '*the French will defend Strasbourg!*' (author's italics).[7]

That done, de Gaulle wrote his last communications of that eventful Monday. He telegraphed both Roosevelt and Churchill, drawing their attention to the extremely serious consequences of any withdrawal, and stressed his opposition to such a move.

Thus it was that the French, still unaware of Eisenhower's decision, were now preparing to embroil him in a first class political row, one which might well split the Western Alliance.

In retrospect it would appear that that Monday, 1 January, 1945, was one of the worst days in Eisenhower's career. But it was more than that. The repercussions of it would, indirectly, last right into our own times; for on that day de Gaulle must have realized that the Americans would not defend European territory, in this case France, if it did not suit their purposes. And he drew his conclusions from that realization when he had firm power in his own hands. He took France out of NATO and his successors have doggedly kept her out ever since. But the French have not been the only Europeans since then to wonder whether the Americans would really fight for European objectives which are not vital to herself. Today there are those in the German Federal Republic, defended in part by that self-same US Seventh Army, who ask: 'Will the Americans really fight for the Bundesrepublik if the Russians ever do come?'

The greenhorns of the 70th Infantry Division were going into the line for the first time. They were to take over Task Force Hudelson's positions, or what was left of them. One month earlier they had been in the States, a world of lights, good food, pretty girls, virtually untouched by the war.

On the outskirts of a little town they had been told was called Philippsbourg, Captain Long told the men of his I Company to drop their big packs. That done, he ordered them to change into combat boots and for the first time the greenhorns realized that 'this was for real'. Elmer Martin of Long's 1st Platoon was not too upset, however. 'I made out as though I was taking off my shoepacs (black felt overshoes used to ward off trench foot), but I didn't. If I was going to die, I'd have dry feet anyway,' he recalled years later.[8]

That night many were going to die, dry feet or otherwise. Strung out in a long line, they began to trudge up the snowy road in the moonlight towards the sound of the firing. Each man was wrapped up in a cocoon of his own thoughts. The usual chatter and good-humoured banter was silenced. Up there, flickering a silent pink like the maws of some gigantic furnace, was the front.

They had just reached the hamlet of Liesbach when Long, at the head of the column, was startled by a harsh '*Halt!*' Immediately he realized the accent wasn't American.

'Hit the dirt!' he yelled. The men scattered into the ditches. On both sides of the road machine guns opened up. Tracer zipped across the snowy road, evil red lights tearing behind it.

In the moonlight Private Martin, mesmerised with horror, saw everything happening 'as in slow motion. Flashes of light to the right and right front. Screams of men. The rapid sound of the enemy's burp and machine guns. The streaks of their tracer. The slow firing of our rifles. . . . You fall, jump, crumble into the ditch and try to get down as far as you can.'[9]

Lieutenant Fillmore, crouched near him in the ditch, tried to call up help. A salvo of slugs ripped the walkie-talkie from his hand.

'Hey, you on the other side of the road,' he cried, 'stop firing. I'm coming over!' With tracer striking the road all around his flying heels, he rushed to safety.

Martin decided he'd do the same. He shook a couple of men lying next to him. They didn't move. They were already dead. Another groaned and said, 'Jesus, God, I hurt!' The wounded man opened his eyes and saw that Martin was preparing to make a dash for it. 'I can't move my legs,' he moaned. '*Please*, don't leave me!'[10]

Martin promised he'd send help, but there was little help coming for the greenhorns that night. He pelted to the other side and dived into the ditch. A Lieutenant Cannon cried, 'How many men left over there?'

Martin fought to catch his breath. 'Sergeant McFuffee, a medic and one wounded, sir,' he gasped. 'The rest are all dead.'

That did it. William Long ordered what was left of his I Company to withdraw. In his first action he had been well and truly 'bushwacked'. The company had suffered three killed, six wounded and fourteen missing, one fifth of its total strength. The greenhorns of the 'Trailblazer Division', as the 70th called itself, had not got off to a good start.

Now Devers was throwing in anyone and everyone. The sagging front had to be shored up until the strategic withdrawal could take place. The man who was given the task of shoring it up was one of the most unusual soldiers America produced in the Second World War – General Frederick, Commander of the 45th Infantry Division. Back in 1943, on the recommendation of an eccentric Englishman, Geoffrey Pyke (some people said he was mad and he did kill himself at the end of the war), the Pentagon set up its mixed-nationality outfit, the 1st Special Forces Brigade. It was composed of rough-tough Canadians and Americans of all kinds – safecrackers, cops, cattle thieves, cowboys, professional gangland assassins. 'The cream of the army and the scum of the stockades,' as someone once called the 1st SF.

Throughout the campaign in Italy this outfit, which one day would lead to the creation of the Green Berets, known to the *Wehrmacht* on account of its daring as the 'Devil's Brigade', was commanded by the then Colonel Robert Frederick; probably no other professional soldier but this slim, vigorous, youthful colonel could have commanded such a tough, hard-to-discipline outfit successfully. Frederick led from the front, being wounded several times, often personally taking patrols behind enemy lines. He was whipcord tough. Once, just after the war, he was having a drink in a West Coast bar when a policeman walked in and asked for his identification card. He didn't believe that such a young man could be wearing the two stars of a major-general. Politely Frederick handed over his ID card. Still the policeman wasn't satisfied. He dropped the card contemptuously on the floor of the bar. Frederick told him to pick it up. The policeman refused. Frederick didn't hesitate. He pole-axed him with a single punch!

The one-time commander of the Devil's Brigade now sought frantically to bolster up the front, with his own troops, tankers from the 12th Armored, Frenchmen from General Leclerc's 2nd French Armored Division, engineers, infantry from the 79th Division and the new boys from the 70th Infantry – in fact anyone who could carry a weapon and was prepared to use it when the Germans came. For Frederick knew that the vital entrance to the Saverne Gap to his rear had to be held at any cost. If it was not and the enemy managed to let loose the armour he was holding ready, there would be little to stop the Germans driving forward to link up with the Colmar Pocket, thus cutting off the whole of the Seventh Army!

One of those who was flung into the hurriedly set-up defence line that night was a young 70th Division infantryman who would one day become a minister of the church. Now he and the rest of his platoon dug in on the hills above Philippsbourg, covering the main road coming from the north, the one the Germans would use.

'Everything seemed quiet,' he recalled forty years later, 'but we began to get anxious when we saw people fleeing down the road with all their possessions stacked high on horse-drawn wagons and hand-pulled carts. We saw fear in their eyes but they were in a hurry and did not stop to talk.'[11]

A German staff car barrelled through their positions before they could stop it. Now the shells from the German 88s started to creep towards the waiting infantrymen. 'Fear gripped us,' the future minister recalls, 'as the 88s came nearer and finally were right on top of us. It is a very helpless feeling, not knowing whether the next shell would have your number on it. . . . Many times during the night we could hear cries of fear and terror, but the men held fast. . . . My Christian faith strengthened me and calmed me at the time because I knew that if I was killed my Lord would take me home and give me eternal life. Many prayers were uttered that night.'[12]

Some were not so sanguine. Sergeant Cloonan, another greenhorn of the 70th Division, who won the Silver and Bronze Stars before the action was over, was in the town itself with some German PoWs when the Germans who had infiltrated the American lines 'started firing on us from all angles. We were under constant shelling from small arms, mortar and artillery fire. . . . Any movement . . . would immediately draw fire.' In the end 'to make room for our own men during the artillery attacks, I ordered the PoWs out of the shelters during artillery attacks . . . and out they would go, shaking in their boots.'[13]

The German PoWs were not the only ones 'shaking in their boots' that night. Some of the American defenders simply could not take the strain. Under cover of darkness they abandoned their positions, leaving gaps through which the most experienced troops in the attack force would sneak on the morrow, the elite Alpine soldiers of the 6th SS Mountain Division. Soon they were to pose the most serious threat to General Frederick's hastily assembled defence.

The 12th SS Regiment of the Sixth, which spearheaded the attack, had come a long way for their first battle with the Americans in the West. Since 1941 they had fought in the swamps, icy marshes, tundra and forests of Finland, aiding the Finns in their battle with the Russians above the Arctic Circle. But in September, 1944, the Russians had finally forced the Finns to surrender. The Sixth had been hurriedly withdrawn by boat, train, truck, sometimes even by sledge. Thereafter there had been a long train journey right across the Reich, hampered and delayed all the time by Allied air attacks.

In spite of its difficulties, the Sixth was up to full strength, the only German division of the whole attack force to be in such a happy state: fifteen thousand vigorous, well-trained young men, experienced in the kind of fighting they were to undergo. If anyone could break through the weary veterans of the 45th and the greenhorns of the 70th and gain the vital passes through the Vosges, it would be the men of the 12th SS Regiment.

As Monday gave way to Tuesday, 900 of them, straight off the train, without any heavy weapons whatsoever, disappeared into the forests, heading for Wingen. As 22-year-old Lieutenant Wolf Zoepf, the adjutant of the 2nd SS Battalion, recalled years later, 'The enemy is in position on both sides of the forest road, with good control over the road. We are without supporting weapons, artillery and mortars. We don't even have steel helmets.'[14]

But, young as he was, Zoepf was a veteran. He and the other officers employed an old trick they had learned in Finland as soon as they spotted the first Americans of the 45th's 179th Regiment. 'We employ our signal pistols with "whistling rounds" which have a good "morale" effect on the enemy.'[15] The Americans fled in some confusion, thinking they were due for a mortar barrage. Behind they left the first 'Ami' prisoners.

The Americans who had saved themselves by 'bugging out' reported to 179th HQ in Wingen that 'meeting opposition, it (the SS regiment) began to support his infantry with *sledge-hammer shelling*' (author's italics).[16] The signal pistols had paid off. The SS men now started to sneak up on Wingen itself.

The commander of the 179th attempted to hold off the Germans and at the same time prepare for withdrawal, as ordered by General Devers, moving his own headquarters prudently to the hamlet of Zittersheim, where the CP of another of Frederick's scratch force of nineteen battalions, the 276th Infantry, was located. 'Terror gripped the civilians,' Madame Anni Mathy recalled. 'Many packed the necessities on their sleds and carts and fled. Since we had cows in the stables, we thought we could not abandon the poor animals and leave them to starve, so we decided to remain.'[17]

Not only the French panicked. In nearby Philippsbourg, also preparing for a German attack, troops were being briefed for combat when a lieutenant asked if he could be excused. Permission was granted. He went outside and immediately shot himself in the foot so that he would not have to fight. An irate colonel ordered the man, writhing in pain on the snow, to be arrested at once. As the *Regimental History* of the 275th Infantry recorded: 'There would be other such cases, here and there.'[18] That day, as Sergeant MacGillivary of the 44th Division became the first soldier in the Seventh Army to win the coveted Medal of Honor in the new battle, there were many cases of bravery and devotion to duty among the men holding the line. But there were others, too, who took the first opportunity they could find to desert their posts and leave their braver comrades in the lurch. Soon, as we shall see, Eisenhower himself would have to step in and stop the rot. For the first time since the Civil War, the US Army was obliged to shoot a man for desertion.

The fate of Strasbourg was nearing its climax. As yet the French did not know that Eisenhower had actually given the order to abandon the

Alsatian capital to the enemy. After the war de Lattre wrote: 'It was unbelievable that nearly thirty hours were to pass before I was told of these vital instructions (the order to withdraw). Souzy himself (the French liaison officer at Devers' HQ), who was at Vittel, knew nothing. The secret of the withdrawal was kept even from our liaison mission. Late in the morning of 2 January, its chief could only report to me the unusual feverishness of certain departments.'[19]

The strain on Eisenhower of trying to maintain the front in both the Ardennes and in Alsace, while at the same time trying to fool his French allies as to his real intentions, was, of course, tremendous. 'This is a very trying period for E,' wrote his secretary-cum-lover Kay Summersby. 'Everyone is feeling a trifle nervous, not knowing exactly where the next attack is coming from. It is up to E all the time to cheer people up. Not an easy job, he can never relax for a moment.'[20]

This Tuesday the attack was coming from his own camp. That afternoon, knowing now what the Americans intended at last, de Gaulle lost no time. He knew just how shaky his provisional government was. France was hopelessly divided between those who had supported Marshal Pétain and thought de Gaulle was a traitor who had broken his oath of loyalty to the state and the supporters of de Gaulle's Free French. There were also many thousands of Communist resistance men probably still armed, waiting to take over if de Gaulle were thrown out. The loss of Alsace, and in particular Strasbourg, would be just the thing they needed.

That afternoon de Gaulle sent General Juin to confirm 'to Eisenhower that France alone would defend Alsace with all the means she had at her disposal'.[21] Juin also said that de Gaulle himself would be visiting Versailles the following day.

Juin had been dealing with the Americans for two years now. Back in November, 1942, he had been the commander-in-chief of Pétain's army in North Africa. Indeed he had ordered his troops to fire on the Americans and their British allies during the landing there. As a result a thousand British and American servicemen had died 'liberating' the French there. Soon after, however, he had gone over to the Allies and had fought with them against the Germans in Tunisia. In December, 1943, he had led the French Expeditionary Corps in Italy. By now he felt he had the measure of the Americans. In a letter to General Giraud, his commander in North Africa, he had written, 'I have the feeling that we will only make our mark here by showing tact and discretion. The Americans are not a people one can hustle. . . . They like us a lot, but they are also imbued with their sense of omnipotence and with a touchiness you can hardly imagine. . . . The French always seem a little excitable to them and it is important for me to first gain their confidence.'[22]

But, in spite of his somewhat cynical appraisal of the Americans, Juin also felt a strong sense of the 'prestige of the French High Command', still smarting from its ignominious defeat in 1940. *La gloire française* meant a lot to him. Now he rode to Versailles, all cynicism tossed to one side, smarting because the Americans appeared to be riding roughshod over French national pride. Not only that, but they had deliberately lied to the French about their intentions in Alsace. In the event, Eisenhower gave the task of handling the angry Frenchman to Bedell Smith. The result was a very stormy discussion indeed.

Juin didn't pull his punches. He told Smith the line must be held at all costs. If it weren't, there would be a bloodbath in Alsace when the Gestapo returned. If Strasbourg were captured, it would be a major propaganda victory for the Germans too. Then he laid it on the line: 'General de Gaulle has ordered de Lattre to take responsibilty for the defence of Strasbourg,' he announced baldly.

Smith's fiery temper, fuelled by a grumbling ulcer, flared. 'If that is so,' he rasped, sticking out his jaw, 'it is bordering on insubordination, pure and simple, *and the French First Army will not get a single further round of ammunition or a gallon of petrol!*'

It was Juin's turn to grow excitable. 'All right,' he snapped. 'In that case General de Gaulle will forbid American forces the use of French railways and communications.'[23]

Bedell Smith at once realized the full implication of what Juin had said. If France cut off their supplies coming up from the Channel ports and Marseilles, all hell would be let loose. He knew that they were heading for a major political row, a public split between two allies. And it couldn't have happened at a worse time. For already Eisenhower was having problems with Montgomery, which would soon escalate into a very serious public row.

Controlling his temper with difficulty, Smith backed off. He agreed that de Gaulle should meet Eisenhower the following day to discuss the matter further. For the time being Juin had won. But later an enraged Bedell Smith told Eisenhower, 'Juin said things to me last night which, if he had been an American, *I would have socked him on the jaw!*'[24]

THREE

It had been a long night in the snowy woods above the small town of Wingen, now occupied by a handful of civilians and some three hundred Americans, including the command post of the 1st Battalion of the 45th Division's 179th Regiment. The SS men, veterans that they were, used the tactics of tension and fear they had seen the Finns employ against the Russians in the wooded tundra of that remote northern country. All night long they had kept their opponents on edge, crying out commands in English, names, insults, yells for help.

Pfc Edson Larson of the 70th Division recalled afterwards: 'The woods were filled with calls from the Germans. *A Company on your feet! Heil Hitler! Down with Roosevelt!* Also much rattling of mess gear. I was with a fellow from Georgia and he said it sounded like a Republican convention!'[1] But this particular 'convention' was going to have a deadly outcome.

Patrolling in the woods that night, Sergeant Richard Struthers of the 70th Division's 276th Infantry, one of the few veterans in the Division, now on his second tour of overseas duty, came across some holes which had been dug recently. Around them someone had placed rocks for further protection. Immediately he knew they were German. He told his company commander, Lieutenant Ivan Stone, but he dismissed the Sergeant's fear. 'Don't worry,' he said airily. 'There are no Germans around here.'[2]

In fact there were nearly a thousand of them lurking in the woods, probing the defences around Wingen, which was to be one of the hot spots of the whole battle on the northern flank of the Seventh Army. Although they were out of touch with the headquarters of the 356th Volksgrenadier Division, to which they were attached, that didn't worry the SS. They were used to acting independently and as SS-men they had great contempt for the infantry of the *Wehrmacht*. They would go it alone. They moved ever closer to the first positions of the unsuspecting men of the 276th Infantry Regiment.

Meanwhile the men of its sister regiment, the 278th, located a dozen or so miles away in the other key village of Philippsbourg, also enjoyed a false sense of security. Admittedly they could hear the soft boom of artillery to their front, but it was a long way away. As it grew lighter there was a deceptive calm about the place.

A medic, T/4 Nelson, recalled years later: 'I visited the latrine and was observing a couple of other medics tinkering with a tire or something on one of the trucks. It seemed like a nice quiet morning when suddenly there were whines and explosions all around.'[3]

The German barrage had begun. Suddenly all was hectic activity. The two doctors took off to help the wounded outside the village. The jeep driver drove away furiously. Abruptly there was the angry chatter of machine guns at close range. Only one of the three medics would return; they had run straight into the attacking Germans.

By midday the village was surrounded and the first German tank was nosing its way cautiously by the little church. An American tank destroyer lumbered into the attack. At once it took up the challenge. Solid armour-piercing shot flashed back and forth. The Third Battalion aidmen fled in disorder. Even the chaplain forgot his customary dignity and made a run for it.

Now the aidmen of the 1st Battalion panicked. Sergeant Place, in charge, yelled, above the thump-thump of the barrage, 'Come on, let's get outa here!'

Nelson objected. 'Where will you go?' he cried. 'We're better off here than out in the woods! Besides, it's against regulations to leave the wounded unattended.' He indicated the half-dozen men moaning and tossing in their blood-stained bandages on the floor.[4]

But it was no use. Most of the medics abandoned the wounded, leaving Nelson, Pfc Piel and an unknown ambulance driver of the 45th Division to tend them.

From outside there came the hollow boom of metal striking metal. They ran to the shattered window. The tank destroyer had been hit. Now it was burning, the crew running for safety under German rifle fire. Suddenly one faltered, his arms flailing the air in his agony, as if he were climbing the rungs of an invisible ladder. Next instant he slipped to the ground. From a nearby house someone yelled urgently 'Medic!'

Nelson hesitated. In the end he asked the 45th man to go along with him, mumbling fearfully that medics weren't supposed to go ahead of the infantry. The 45th veteran rounded upon him hotly. 'Those fellows are doing the fighting in this war,' he snarled at the greenhorn. 'The least we can do is to pick them up when they're hurt!'[5]

The Germans were everywhere in Philippsbourg now. The American command lost control. The men were isolated in houses and cellars, fighting back as best they could in little groups.

'Hell, it's hotter here than in Anzio!' an ambulance driver of the 45th Division yelled to Pfc Mulholland of the 70th.[6]

Private Herbert Thiesen ran out of his house to find ammunition; his hard-pressed little group were running low. He didn't get far. German fire struck him almost at once and he hit the ground hard. A medic ran out to help. Moments later he scampered back gasping that Thiesen was dead. But the dead man wouldn't lie down. To their surprise the men saw him stagger to his feet and struggle to the nearest house. The bullet which had felled him had penetrated his helmet, gone through his right temple and exited behind his right ear, without doing any serious damage!

He was one of the fortunate ones. Casualties were mounting rapidly in the 1st Battalion Aid Post where Nelson was in charge. The 45th driver volunteered to run the gauntlet of German fire to evacuate the wounded, although his ambulance was already riddled with bullet holes.

Now Nelson was faced with a new trial. The ambulance only held four wounded. Who should go? All around him the men on the floor begged to be taken as the Germans crept ever nearer. Nelson remained calm. He made his first choice—a boy who had been blinded. Gently he guided him outside towards the ambulance.

Fortunately, at this time Captain Ferree, one of the missing doctors, struggled in. He pitched in immediately, beginning operating straight away with the assistance of one of the medics who had been wounded and had risen from his own stretcher to help.

A sergeant was brought in, one leg practically blown off. Ferree did the preliminary cutting and one of the medics completed the operation by severing the leg with bandage scissors. Another popular NCO, Sergeant Smith, was brought in, badly injured in leg and shoulders. Ferree decided to amputate to save Smith's life. Hastily the leg was removed. Long afterwards Nelson remembered: 'The amputated leg with the combat boot still on it was deposited next to the door, where it made a gruesome sight when the door was shut. We left the door open as much as possible.'[7]

As Wingen also came under attack from the SS, the threat to the 44th Division on the Seventh Army's front in the Bitche area became acute. To bolster up the sagging line General Patch ordered up the US 255th Infantry and, perhaps the most controversial outfit in his whole command, General Leclerc's famed 2nd French Armored Division.

Back in 1940 Captain Vicomte Philippe de Hautecloque, a wounded and hunted man, had sworn he would not surrender like most of his comrades in the beaten French Army. He had smuggled himself out of France to join de Gaulle in England. Within weeks he was fighting again in Africa, where he achieved the first victory of Free French arms at the remote oasis of Kufra in Central Africa. There, after the Italian garrison had surrendered to him and he had begun his long march to join Montgomery's British in Egypt, he had written to de Gaulle: 'We will not rest until the flag of France also flies over Paris and Strasbourg.'

Montgomery had taken to him at once when he turned up in Egypt after an incredible march over hundreds of miles, looking 'as you might say you had dropped over from the next village to tea,' as Freddie de Guingand, Montgomery's Chief-of-Staff, recorded. Montgomery shook the emaciated Frenchman's hand and later told de Guingand, 'I can make use of that chap.'[8]

The Americans had made use of him too. Under the pseudonym of Leclerc, (under his own name he had been sentenced to death by Pétain's Vichy government as a traitor and he feared reprisals against his family who were still in France) he had captured Paris under Patton's command and then, three months later, he had made an unorthodox and unauthorized dash through the Vosges to capture Strasbourg itself. He had kept the promise of what had become known as the 'Oath of Kufra'. But in November, 1944, when he captured the Alsatian capital, he had told Devers 'he would not go down to join the First French Army guarding the Colmar Pocket.' He would not fight with Juin, de Lattre and the rest of those officers who had served Pétain loyally until the tide of the war had turned. As Devers recorded later: 'I just couldn't get Leclerc to join the French 1st Army . . . so I sent him back (to the Seventh).'[9] To Wade Haislip, commander of the US XV

Corps, whom Leclerc trusted and regarded as something of a father figure, Leclerc said: 'I want you to tell General Devers something from me. It is that I, myself, and every man in my division are volunteers. We do not have to fight . . . but we do it for the liberation and honour of France. But if he ever attaches us to the divisions of de Lattre we will pack up and go home.'[10]

Now, just as Leclerc prepared to lead his men into the attack, he was handed an official-looking envelope. He read through its contents and then threw back his head 'and laughed and laughed and laughed,' as his aide, Colonel Chatel recalls.[11] But it was bitter cynical laughter. Without a word he handed the letter to the Colonel. It was from the French Supreme Court stating that General Leclerc d'Hautecloque had been reprieved; his death sentence had been rescinded. As Chatel said later, 'Despite all the magnificent things Leclerc had done for France, despite all the honours he had won, the new régime in Paris had found it necessary to proceed through official channels and lift the death sentence. . . . This was the reason for the bitterness of the joke as he saw it.'[12]

This bitter division among the French people clearly decided de Gaulle to go to Versailles to press his case for the abandonment of the withdrawal in Alsace. Churchill arrived from London and the conference between him, de Gaulle and Eisenhower began.

Eisenhower was not in a particularly good mood that Wednesday lunchtime. The news from Alsace was bad and his offer of pardons to the many thousands of US soldiers in stockades through the ETO (European Theatre of Operations) if they would take up arms had been disappointing. Only a few score of the rapists, thieves and deserters had taken up his offer. He had a guilty conscience as well. He had not written to his wife, Mamie, since Christmas and every time he walked into his office he saw the photo of her and his son John on his desk. Soon he was to write to her: 'From your papers you will understand that it is hard to sit down and compose thoughts applicable to a letter to one's best only girl.'[13] He hoped that the letter would soft-soap Mamie enough for her not to send him one of those griping letters which he feared and hated. Plagued by such professional and private worries, Eisenhower was not in a particularly good frame of mind to play the role on which he prided himself – that of mediator between warring factions within the great military alliance. In the event, it seems that the Great Old Man, sitting there like a pink Buddha, puffing away at his majestic cigar, did the mediating.

Eisenhower opened by explaining his poor situation in the Ardennes, the problem of the Colmar Pocket and his shortage of manpower. 'That is why I have ordered the troops to establish another, shorter line further back.'

'If we were at Kriegsspiel,' retorted de Gaulle, 'I would say you were right. But I must consider the matter from another point of view. Retreat in Alsace would yield French territory to the enemy. In the realm of strategy this would be only a manoeuvre. But for France it would be a national disaster. At the present moment we are concerned with Strasbourg. I have ordered the First French Army to defend the city. It will, therefore, do so in any case. But it would be deplorable if this entailed a dispersion of Allied forces, perhaps even a rupture in the system of command. That is why I urge you to reconsider your plan to order General Devers to hold fast in Alsace.'

Eisenhower frowned when he heard that delicately phrased 'rupture in the system of command' translated by the interpreter. He knew what de Gaulle was hinting at, namely that France and the French Army might go it alone. De Gaulle thought 'the Supreme Commander seemed impressed'.

'You give political reasons for me to change military orders,' objected Eisenhower.

'Armies,' de Gaulle answered loftily, 'are created to serve the policy of states. And no one knows better than you yourself that strategy should include not only the given circumstances of military technique, but also the moral elements. And for the French people and the French soldiers, the fate of Strasbourg is of extreme moral importance.'

Just as Eisenhower had lectured Bedell Smith a few days before, now he too was being lectured, and not only by de Gaulle, but also by Churchill, who said, 'All my life I have remarked what significance Alsace has for the French. I agree with General de Gaulle that this fact must be taken into consideration.'

Still Eisenhower did not give in. He pointed out that if the French went it alone, he might cut off their fuel and ammunition supplies, but de Gaulle wasn't impressed by this attempt at blackmail. He made Juin's point once more that France would forbid the use of the French communication system by the American Army, adding, 'Rather than contemplate the consequences of such possibilities I felt I should rely on General Eisenhower's strategic talent and on his devotion to the service of the coalition of which France constituted a part.'

Eisenhower gave in. He telephoned Devers to cancel the retreat at once. The withdrawal of General Brooks' VI Corps should be limited so that its right wing would go on holding on to Alsatian territory some distance north of the Alsatian capital. Strasbourg was saved.

That done, Eisenhower told de Gaulle he would send Bedell Smith to Devers the following day with these orders in writing, but de Gaulle was taking no chances. As he wrote later, 'I agreed with Eisenhower that Juin should accompany Bedell Smith which would be an additional guarantee for me and for the executants, proof that agreement had been reached.'

Over the tea which followed, Eisenhower confessed to de Gaulle that he was having problems with his Allied subordinates. 'At this very moment,' he complained, 'I am having a lot of trouble with Montgomery, a general of great ability, but a bitter critic and a mistrustful subordinate.'

'Glory has its price,' de Gaulle said airily, and then tried to sweeten the pill of defeat. 'Now you are going to be a conqueror!'

Outside the Petit Trianon Juin said to de Gaulle that he felt Churchill deserved a word of thanks. After all, he *had* indicated as soon as they entered the conference room 'that everything had been arranged'.[14]

'Bah!' was de Gaulle's reply and as the car drew up and they entered, he slumped in the back seat in gloomy contemplation.

That night Eisenhower wrote to his boss, Marshall, in Washington: 'All my life I have known what significance Alsace had for the French. I agree with de Gaulle that this fact must be taken into consideration.'

Despite Eisenhower's decision to stop the retreat, the Germans pressed home their advantage in a series of bitter clashes all along the front. At Philippsbourg on 3 January, Private George Turner of the 14th Armored Division, belonging to another of those scratch battalions thrown in by Frederick, was cut off from his artillery outfit. He joined a friendly infantry company withdrawing under heavy fire. Suddenly he spotted two German tanks followed by seventy-five German infantrymen. Though not trained for this kind of combat, he grabbed a rocket launcher and went to meet the Germans. They spotted him and he came under immediate small arms and cannon fire. But he held his ground. Standing in the middle of the road, slugs cutting the air all around him, he aimed and fired. The first tank came to a halt, flames pouring from it. Turner fired again and the other halted, badly damaged. He wasn't finished yet. He flung away the bazooka.

Running to an abandoned half-track, he dismantled its machine gun and, standing there like John Wayne in a western shoot-out, he sprayed the Germans with half-inch bullets. The attack came to an abrupt halt and the Americans went over to the offensive. The Germans brought up 75mm anti-tank cannon. The American Shermans, supporting the infantry, came under fire. Two were hit and came to a halt. Again Turner went into action, while the crews of the tanks pelted for safety. One tanker couldn't make it and was trapped. Suddenly the Sherman, known among the troops as 'the Ronson lighter' on account of the ease with which it caught fire, burst into flames. Turner didn't hesitate. He dropped his machine gun and doubled towards the blazing tank. Desperately he tried to rescue the trapped tanker. There was a muffled roar as the Sherman's ammunition locker exploded. Turner was thrown to the ground, painfully wounded. Still he refused to be evacuated. As his citation read: 'He remained with the infantry until the following day, driving off an enemy patrol with serious casualties, assisting in capturing a hostile strongpoint and voluntarily and fearlessly driving a truck through heavy enemy fire to deliver wounded men to the rear aid station.'[15]

George Turner, the artilleryman turned infantryman, was later awarded his country's highest honour, the Medal of Honor.

The future minister, Pfc Docken, who had spent the previous night sleeping with some cows in a stable near Philippsbourg, knew now that he had frostbite. But then 'all of us had a little frostbite, but those fellows with feet that sweat easily had the most trouble'.[16]

But the greenhorns of the 70th Division were learning fast and were now keeping a spare pair of socks 'in our bosom' so they had dry warm socks to change into, pressing the wet pair taken off close to their body to dry out. They learned how to cut the tails off their heavy greatcoats which soon became soaked with the snow and froze. They learned how to urinate on their frozen weapons to de-freeze the mechanism. They learned how to interchange their sweat-soaked shirts, wearing them two at a time for extra warmth, the wet one closest to the body being replaced by the dry outer one.

It was little better for the attacking Germans. Young Lieutenant Zoepf of the 6th SS recalled later how, as it started to grow dark that night, 'Our packtrain arrives with ammunition and rations – half a loaf of bread and some spreading for each man. Our men are told: "To get their next rations from the enemy; no further supply."

'Now they march again, slogging through the knee-deep snow. . . . We are exhausted from the lack of sleep. Every little stop on our march is immediately used for sleep, leaning on a tree, crouching or sitting. . . . The pace is killing.'[17] But there was to be no respite for the exhausted underfed mountain men of the Sixth SS. On the morrow Wingen had to be taken, cost what it may.

The suffering went on and on. That month a reporter from the army newspaper, *Stars and Stripes*, recorded what it was like at a Seventh Army casualty clearing centre behind the front: 'They chased some kids out of the narrow courtyard so that the ambulance could back up and unload. Two of the passengers were walking wounded. The third was a litter case, a young lieutenant all doped up with morphine.

' "He thinks he's still up front," said the driver. "All the way he kept yelling something about a machine gun on a hill and kept repeating, 'We've got to attack; we've got to attack!' " It was cold outside and the driver shivered a little. "The first guy we ever hauled from the front was like that," said the driver. "He had his brains wrapped up in bandages and I expected him to start screaming at any minute because it was the roughest cross-country trip I ever made." But the driver's assistant, the aptly named Tristan Coffin of the 103rd Infantry Division, said quietly, "I don't remember them any more. They're all just faces to me . . . and some of them don't even have faces." '[18]

FOUR

The men of Colonel Wallace Cheves' Battalion of the 274th Infantry Regiment who were going to try and help their hard-pressed comrades at Wingen arrived at the front worn and tired. Bedding down on the hard floors of a local factory just over the hill from Wingen, they mixed with the survivors of the 70th and 45th Divisions who had escaped from the débâcle.

Colonel Cheves remembered his first impressions of that meeting between his greenhorns and these new veterans: 'We thought we'd had it tough, but these men looked worse. Their faces were haggard and worn and drawn from lack of sleep and deeply lined from recent horrible experiences. Most were in their early twenties, but they looked like men of thirty-five or forty years old. They were dirty, unshaven and stinking of sweat. None of them wanted to talk about the things they had seen or the hardships they had endured. The actuality of the war was very close upon us now.'[1]

On that Thursday, four days after the German attack had begun, yet another American·battalion was thrown in to experience its baptism of fire as Cheves' battalion set off towards Wingen. None of them, not even the Colonel, knew what the true situation at Wingen was. Obviously the Germans had attacked there. The survivors of the 45th and 70th had admitted that, but were they still holding the place? Had some of the American defenders stayed behind and slogged it out? Were the silent, haggard men they had mixed with simply stragglers or even cowards who had just 'bugged out' and left the 200 Americans, still unaccounted for, to fight on?

So they marched on in silence. Some of them had been training for years for this moment. How were they going to react when the silence was broken by that first burst of enemy fire?

Colonel Wallace Cheves, a thoughtful and sensitive officer, recalled later: 'Our hearts and minds harboured many things we would like to have said, but somehow we knew it was better to remain silent. This was the moment we had often wondered about, secretly dreaded. Our faces were set and there was a faraway look in everybody's eyes.'[2]

The sounds of battle started to grow louder as they laboured through the snow. Then there was Wingen lying silent below them. It was like a scene from a cheap Christmas card – medieval, half-timbered houses, their steep roofs covered with snow, huddled round the church. Only a thin trail of brown smoke rising from a chimney here and there indicated that it was still inhabited. Where were the SS? Had they already left, taking their two hundred-odd American prisoners from the 45th and 70th Divisions with them? What *was* going on in Wingen?

The SS men of the Sixth Mountain Division had come sneaking into Wingen that morning. Here and there the Americans had not been caught off their guard and there had been some heavy firing. But for the most part the GIs of the 70th and 45th Divisions were caught by surprise. Corporal Ben Stein of the 45th was one. Veteran of Anzio as he was, his carbine had not been fired for some time and was encrusted with dirt. Now as he peered through the window of the house where he and some other service troops had been sleeping, he saw young SS men triumphantly escorting American prisoners, hands clasped behind their heads. He and the others decided to lie low. But suddenly rifle fire exploded to the front and rear of the house in which they were hiding. A voice thundered in accented English, 'Americans, come out with your hands high!'

'We laid down our guns and filed out. The dead man from our platoon lay a few feet away. A German machine gun was set up across the street and white-coated Krauts were standing around with rifles and machine pistols aimed at us. They looked tough and menacing and some had cigarettes dangling from their lips. I figured this was the end of the line.'[3]

For some it was. They were not maltreated, though they were relieved of their watches, cigarettes and the like. Then they were marched to the church, Ben Stein stumbling over the dead body of a GI in the process. 'When we started up the front steps, one of our men bent over to tie up his boot. He was shot immediately. I was shocked, but walked on past the dead body, sprawled on the church steps. We were herded down the stairs to the church cellar where we joined about a hundred or more other prisoners. There was very little water or food and German guards were in sight at all times. Buckets were placed around as makeshift latrines. No one moved out of that cellar. There was nothing to do except sleep – and wait.'[4]

Over 400 Americans were rounded up by the SS, and while the officers made their dispositions for the expected American counterattack, their men 'feasted on captured US rations,' as Lieutenant Zoepf recalled, 'resupplying their losses in clothing and taking American rifles to supplement their weapons.'[5]

But in spite of their success, the SS had problems too. As Erich Meyer, a machine gunner in the 1st SS Battalion records: 'We hadn't slept for days and were exhausted and hungry. . . . We were astonished to see how well American soldiers lived.'[6] But food and sleep were not their only problems. No one in the German High Command knew of the SS's capture of Wingen. As Lieutenant Zoepf remembers, 'Our signalmen were not successful in establishing any sort of radio contact with Corps. Neither was the forward observer of the 3rd Battalion, Mountain Artillery Regiment *Nord*.'[7] Patrols were hurriedly dispatched to the rear to carry the good news to Corps, for when the Americans counterattacked, the surviving SS men would be completely dependent upon their own resources and the two captured Ami self-propelled guns they had put into service. Already up in the hills the SS could hear the rumble of enemy tanks.

While Cheves' men waited above Wingen, their comrades of the 274th Regiment's First Battalion, under the command of Colonel Willis, were preparing to attack Philippsbourg. First they were to capture the hills around the place and then clear the enemy out of the village. There was a last check of equipment. Frozen and tired after the long truck journey, the infantrymen formed up into skirmish lines. Here and there company commanders gave the order, 'Fix bayonets.'

'Let's go!' was the next order. Machine guns opened up. There was the clatter of tank tracks. Heavy guns boomed.

Lieutenant Vaught's A Company on the right was running through the snow towards a hill Willis had ordered them to capture. Almost immediately the Germans spotted them and the SS cannon began firing.

'I never understood how they ever got across that open space,' a man in the watching C Company reported later. 'It was horrible to watch. The earth erupted almost continously as shell after shell plastered the ground around them. But they never faltered – just kept going, leaving dead and wounded behind. I could see men flung into the air, hit the ground, roll over and lie still, deathly still. Some just disintegrated before my eyes.'[8] The infantry were paying the price of de Gaulle's intervention.

'We were having a tough time,' recalled Sergeant Durgan of A Company, 'but, in spite of the disastrous fire, most of us made it across to the foot of the first hill. Here we had protection from the high-angle artillery fire, but still the hill was alive with Krauts who kept shooting away.'[9]

The brave survivors of A Company now tried to storm the hill but intense small arms fire drove them back. They broke into small groups, fighting back as best they could. Among them was medic Pfc Horton. He kept on tending the wounded, crying to the ashen-faced infantrymen lying in the snow, trying to pluck up courage for another go. One of them, Pfc Donald Eddy, was infected by Horton's spirit. He yelled at the frightened men all around him, 'Pass out the crap paper, boys!'[10]

Lieutenant Vaught's men tried another approach. Instead of a frontal attack, they attempted to go round the hill and come up in the rear of the Germans. Cautiously the infantry moved forward through the firs. But suddenly a German popped up from a foxhole. It seemed as if he was about to surrender so the Americans motioned him forward. As he did so, another German sprang from his hiding place, stick grenade raised. The Americans were quicker off the mark. He went down riddled with bullets but Vaught now decided to let the big guns blast out the Germans. Round after round crashed into the hill, the earth shaking beneath the feet of the waiting infantrymen. Then they were moving forward once more and this time they took the hill without difficulty.

While A Company had been attacking, Captain Jack Wallace's C Company had been advancing on the left down the railway track towards the village. Suddenly they came under fire and the inexperienced troops, thinking it was their own artillery firing short, sent out a call for the American batteries to lift their fire. The puzzled answer came back, 'We're not firing.' They were under German fire for the first time.

Under Lieutenant Brogan, a squad dashed forward to probe for a weak spot. The Germans soon spotted the scouts, who came under intense fire. For a while they were pinned down. But Brogan's Irish temper flared and he took off 'like a big bird', as Pfc Jones recalled. He dashed towards a nearby house and set up a fire base there to cover the advance of his stalled company.

Now C Company was moving once more, dashing from house to house in a series of spurts. A pillbox stopped them and Pfc Lloyd was ordered to grenade it. As he complained later, 'I don't know why in hell they always picked on me when they wanted a shitty job done. Well, anyway, there were Jones and I crawling right up to this pillbox. We were all set to throw out grenades when a Kraut came out waving a white flag.'[11]

Pfc de Wald, who 'spoke the Kraut lingo', asked their prisoner if there were any more Germans inside and to his surprise eighteen more men emerged. Just at that moment the enemy opened fire on the little party. Two Americans and three Germans went down in a confused mess of shattered limbs. The other Germans then decided they didn't want to surrender after all and tried to use the grenades they had concealed about them. The GIs were quicker. Pfc Kirk dropped one with a shot between the eyes. His grenade exploded in his hands, blowing him to pieces.

The cost of this little advance down a street which in normal circumstances might have taken two minutes to walk was high. Out of the original twelve, only four were left. Dying in the snow, Pfc Kious, his body riddled with tracer bullets, croaked. 'Those darn tracers burn a guy's guts out. Have you any water?' He died with the cry 'mother' on his parched lips.[12]

B Company had advanced on the decks of some Sherman tanks. Already they had suffered a few casualties from German artillery fire. Now they were almost approaching their objective when a dozen planes came out of the sky with startling suddenness. One of the men recognized them as American. 'They're friendly,' he yelled, but the words died on his lips as two of them peeled off and started shooting up the artillery positions just behind them. 'Chunks of steel were flying around like snow,' he recalled, 'the fragments clipping the limbs of trees. A piece of shrapnel struck my helmet and my ears rang for thirty minutes.'[13] He hit the ground with the rest of the survivors and crawled into a nearby ditch. Nevertheless he was glad to spend the rest of the day there in hiding.

The attackers were going to ground almost everywhere in and

around Philippsbourg and for the first time the American soldiers were observing the strange effects that violent action could have on quite normal young men. Sergeant Kelsey of B Company was just carrying a wounded NCO into a barn for treatment when he observed a soldier named Applegate attempting to set up his mortar when it was shattered by enemy fire. 'If you have ever seen a man freeze in place, well, that is just what he did. He just froze bending and couldn't go any further. Then as if a thunderbolt had struck him, he straightened up and ran like a wildcat for the barn.'[14]

Now, as Colonel Cheves, the historian of the 70th Infantry Division, observed later, 'The battle for Phillippsbourg was no longer a battle of opposing infantrymen. It had developed into a duel of death between the big guns on both sides.'[15] All that January afternoon the guns thundered back and forth as the infantry bogged down.

At Wingen Colonel Cheves' Battalion had begun its attack, but already the Germans holding the ridges above the town were ripping into their ranks with machine guns, so cunningly concealed that the GIs had almost walked into them. One of the surprised infantrymen rallied immediately. As his CO wrote later, 'Sergeant Hughie Shellem wasn't afraid of anything. He yelled, "Let's go and get 'em, just like we did in basic training!" He darted forward. To his front in the trees he spotted a German machine gun. He whipped out a grenade and threw it. The gun ceased firing abruptly.'

Suddenly Shellem stopped, turned, and fell. He had been hit.

'Medics!' someone yelled.

A medic dashed forward. He had just reached Shellem when he, too, was hit. Shellem yelled, 'Break open a case of Purple Hearts, guys. They've got me in the tail!'[16]

They were the last words he ever uttered. His fighting career was over minutes after it had started. He died there in the snow where he had fallen.

The attack started to bog down. As Cheves recorded later: 'We were in a tough spot lying there in the snow while the unseen enemy blazed away about fifty yards to our front.'[17] But the Colonel hadn't reckoned with young Lieutenant Cassidy about whose ability to lead men in action he had previously had some doubts. The 22-year-old officer, who was a devout Catholic, had 'no fear of dying as I had made my peace with God. However I had great apprehension that I would not measure up to what was expected of me as a soldier and leader of men.'[18]

He sprang to his feet and someone yelled, 'Lieutenant Cassidy, you'd better keep down, you're going to get killed standing up there!'[19] Cassidy paid no heed. He just hunched his shoulders and went forward. His courage inspired the battalion. The mortarmen began to blast the German positions on the ridge. Even before the final round had landed, they were up and charging the Germans, who now began to fall back. In short order they cleaned out the woods and were ready for the new day's attack on Wingen.

But even now the Germans displayed their greater experience. As Cassidy led his men through the woods, they came across a small house in a clearing. One of his squad leaders, Sergeant Wexler, saw someone waving a white flag in the gloom. He stood up, ordering his men not to fire, and called to the Germans in their own language to come out with their hands up. But it was the old, old trick. In that same instant a German machine gun opened up to the flank. Sergeant Wexler and several of his men fell. The trick had worked and the GIs had learned another bitter lesson. As another freezingly cold night fell on the wooded heights above Wingen, the men of the 70th Division told themselves grimly, as they squatted in their foxholes: 'The only good Kraut is a dead Kraut.'

They were not the only ones tricked that bitter January day. Leclerc's veterans of the 2nd French Armored Divison had now arrived at the front, split up into small combat groups in the Bitche salient. Advancing in a blizzard in support of American infantry, they were about to open fire on some tanks to their front when they realized they were American Shermans. Immediately the tank gunners, straining their eyes against the flying snow, relaxed their grips on the firing handles, telling themselves another US tank outfit had somehow taken over the point. Or perhaps they were retreating before a Boche attack?

Neither was the case. Suddenly the lead Sherman's 75mm cannon spat fire. At that range the other Sherman couldn't miss. The first of Leclerc's tanks reeled to a sudden stop. It began to blaze immediately. The French had been caught out by an old Boche trick. The Germans had led their own column with a captured Sherman, still bearing the familiar white star of the Allied invasion force. The triumphant Germans surged forward, pouring fire into the stalled French tanks from all sides. Other Germans, dressed in US uniforms and driving captured jeeps, whipped in and out of the French column, tossing grenades to left and right and vanished into the whirling snow before the French knew what was happening to them.

Caught completely by surprise, their casualties mounting by the minute, the victors of Paris, Strasbourg and half a score of other battles, knew there was no future for them here. There was only one way out of this bloody confusion. Leclerc's men fled.

As the fighting began to die down, with the Germans seemingly victorious everywhere, there seemed to be confusion and trickery at all levels of command in the US Seventh Army. From top to bottom nothing seemed to be going right.

Near Wingen an embattled Colonel Cheves, weary and sick, discovered that yet again there was no hot food for his exhausted men. Too sick to look into the matter himself, he sent his hot-headed executive officer, Major Boyd, to find out why. Minutes later Major Boyd strode into Cheves' CP, choking with rage.

'Do you know what I found out when I went back to check on those kitchen trucks?' he yelled. 'I'll tell you. The whole goddam bunch of them were just sitting there, not doing a damn thing! Half of them were asleep. And you know what that supply officer of ours was doing? He was sitting there *eating*! I told him if I ever caught his ass around here again, *I'd shoot him on sight!*'[20]

At the highest level, too, confusion, even chaos, appeared to reign. The Germans' real intentions seemed unclear, in spite of Ultra. Although it had been decided thirty hours ago that de Lattre's French First Army would take over the defence of Strasbourg and the sector along the Rhine further north, nothing as yet had been seen of the French troops. The line of the Rhine was being held to north and south of Strasbourg, extending some *twenty-nine* miles, by five lone infantry battalions of Task Force Linden! Now some of these battalions were being thinned out even further since General Patch expected the French to begin taking over the sector. Although Sixth Army Group had warned Patch it would take a 'tremendous effort' for the French to take over by midnight on 5 January, Patch still carried out his orders. He began to withdraw his troops from the Rhine so that by the evening of the Fourth, he had the equivalent of two regiments, some six thousand men, defending a front which had been extended to *thirty-one miles*! It was a recipe for disaster, as a totally new threat began to loom on the horizon.

In Strasbourg itself the US Third Infantry Division, which had been guarding the Alsatian capital, had departed in accordance with the new plan. Now, apart from a few raw French territorials, all that remained there of the US Army was Task Force Linden's postal officer, a port company of US Engineers and three men who produced a divisional newspaper!

It was not surprising that Charles Frey, the Senior Mayor of Strasbourg, decided it was time to send a belated Christmas card to General de Lattre lying sick in bed in his hotel HQ. Once again he had been stricken by the old congestion of the lungs, a result of being gassed as a young lieutenant in the First World War. The card bore a picture of Strasbourg's famed single-towered Gothic cathedral and it bore these solemn words: 'To General de Lattre, our only hope.'[21]

That night in his primitive aid station at Niederbronn, Major Ezra I. Silver, the 275th Infantry Regiment's regimental surgeon, was busy working his way through the casualties from the day's fighting in nearby Philippsbourg. He worked flat out, trying to keep up with the ever-increasing flow of torn young bodies, the floor slippery with blood, the bins overflowing with amputated limbs. With the medics were chaplains of all denominations, trying to calm the fears of the wounded, comforting them the best they could. One of the chaplains was the Baptist Minister D. B. Webber, an officer Silver did not particularly like. Silver had always thought of him 'as a very stiff and unyielding person'. Now he was with the surgeon as he completed the treatment of a young infantryman who had been badly wounded in the abdomen and leg. Silver had pumped the boy full of morphine and, as the pain wore off, the young soldier opened his eyes and said to the surgeon, 'Have you got a cigarette, Doc?' To Silver's surprise, Webber, who had always lectured the men on the vices of drinking, gambling and smoking, took a packet of cigarettes out of his own pocket, placed one between the lips of the wounded man and held a lighted match to it. The boy took a few drags of the cigarette.

Silver watched fascinated at this transformation in the Baptist chaplain. Suddenly, however, 'every muscle in the boy's body tensed. His eyes rolled back and in a moment, he had passed on – from a blood clot which had reached his lung.'[22]

Ashen-faced, the Baptist chaplain went out of the aid station and, leaning against the wall outside, broke down and wept.

PART II

Crisis

'I count upon you to enable me to announce to
the Führer in a few days' time that the swastika
flag flies again over Strasbourg Cathedral.'
Order of the Day,
Himmler's Army of the Upper Rhine,
5 January, 1945

ONE

He had always wanted to be a soldier, a leader of men. As a boy in his native Munich he had volunteered for the Bavarian Army immediately he came of age. In a training battalion he had made it as far as officer-cadet, but, to his chargin, the First World War ended before he could be sent to the Western Front. Thereafter his 'combat experience' had been limited to those notorious *Saalschlachten* (beerhouse brawls) that the Party, which he had joined almost immediately it had been founded, constantly fought with its political opponents. But even there he could not gain the decorations he so coveted. Try as he might in those nightly brawls with the communists and socialists, he never seemed able to qualify for the Party's *Blutordnen* (Order of the Blood) granted to those National Socialists who had had their head split open or nose broken by some Red wielding a beer mug!

By 1945, after five years of war, the second most powerful man in the Third Reich had one single decoration adorning his skinny chest, the Sports Medal in Bronze – and even that had taken some doing for the weedy *Reichsführer*! On 10 December, 1944, however, the man who lusted for the Knight's Cross, was granted his first army command by a grateful Führer. Heinrich Himmler, the head of the Reich's dreaded police *apparat* and the one-million-strong Armed SS, was given command of Army Group Upper Rhine. That meant he was in control of all forces on the opposite bank of the Rhine and of General Wiese's 19th Army surrounded in the Colmar Pocket.

Hostile critics such as Colonel-General Guderian, head of the *Wehrmacht's* Armoured Force, were appalled. He wrote later: 'He (Himmler) harboured no doubts about his own importance. He believed that he possessed powers of military judgment every bit as good as Hitler's and needless to say far better than those of the generals.'¹ Guderian felt that Himmler 'completely underestimated the qualities that are necessary for a man to be a successful commander of troops. On the very first occasion when he had to undertake a task before the eyes of the world – one that could not be carried out by means of backstairs intrigues and fishing in troubled waters – the man inevitably proved a failure. It was complete irresponsibility on his part to wish to hold such an appointment; it was equally irresponsible of Hitler to entrust him with it.'²

Now the sallow-faced Himmler, who looked like a provincial teacher with his pince-nez and prissy little clipped moustache, decided that the time had come to take advantage of the confusion reigning in Devers' command on the opposite bank of the Rhine. His spies had kept him well informed of the situation in Strasbourg. He knew that the US 3rd Infantry Division had gone and that the town was now defended by a motley crew of ill-armed French irregulars, grandly named the 'Guards.' He knew, too, that the whole length of the Rhine was virtually wide-open, some sectors being solely patrolled by American reconnaissance units, the front being thinned all the time as Devers moved troops to the hard-pressed northern flank and de Lattre's French failed to fill the gaps. The situation was ripe for exploitation. From the north Blaskowitz's Army Group, G, already heavily engaged in the lower Vosges, would make another thrust. This time it would be armoured: a three-division attack driving in the general direction of Wissembourg. Simultaneously, in the south, Himmler's 19th Army would break out of the Colmar Pocket. There the 198th Infantry Division and the *Feldherrnhalle* armoured brigade would attack towards Benfeld.

While all this was going on, Himmler would launch a *third* operation. His 553rd Volksgrenadier Division was to make an assault crossing of the Rhine at Gambsheim. Himmler reasoned, as did Hitler, that if all these drivers linked up successfully, the whole of Northern Alsace would be cut off. If they failed and the advance westwards was stopped, at least Strasbourg would be reconquered. What a tremendous shot in the arm it would be for the German people if Himmler could announce that Strasbourg was German again on that most significant day in the yearly calendar of the National Socialist Party – 30 January, 1945, the twelfth anniversary of Hitler's take-over of power in 1933!

Although Ultra had long alerted Devers to the fact that the Germans might attempt another surprise attack elsewhere along his huge front, the commander of Sixth Army Group was caught by surprise. For days now General Linden's defence of the Rhine in the Gambsheim area had been limited to daily reconnaissance patrols run by the 94th Mechanized Reconnaissance Squadron of the 12th Armored Division. These motorized patrols were sent out to check the riverside villages, most of them pro-German, and sweep along the banks of the Rhine. On the early morning of the 5th one such patrol failed to return at the appointed time. Hastily another patrol of armoured cars and half-tracks was organized and sent to the same area. They soon came back, bringing with them alarming news. The Germans had made a surprise crossing of the Rhine the previous night, gaining footholds at Gambsheim and further on at Herrlisheim, most of whose farmers were definitely pro-German!

Surprisingly enough the Commanding General of the 12th Armored Division did nothing. Nor did higher headquarters. According to the *Divisional History* of the Twelfth: 'Higher headquarters was apparently convinced that this force was small and of inferior quality and that its mission was merely to occupy the ground the Allies would give up in their anticipated withdrawal to the Vosges mountains.'[3] As a result the 'Hellcats', as the men of the 12th liked to call themselves, were not alerted for a counterattack until the morning of 6 January. That 'small and inferior' force was going to give the 'Hellcats' a bloody baptism of fire they would remember for the rest of their fighting career.

Meanwhile Himmler, jubilant at the lack of opposition, continued to build up his bridgehead, ferrying over not only the infantry, but elements of the very experienced 21st Panzer Division, which had taken the first brunt of the Allied landings in Normandy the previous June. It seemed that another disaster in Alsace was in the making.

The US 79th Infantry Division, the 'Cross of Lorraine' as it was known from its divisional insignia, was another of Devers' few veteran formations. Formed in June, 1942, it had gone into action for the first time in August, 1944, fighting its way under Patton's command right across France. In spite of the fact that its commander, General Ira Wyche, had been wounded in the leg right at the outset of the campaign, he had set a cracking pace and had led the Division in its assault crossing of the Seine.

Up to now the Division had not been involved in any really serious fighting in the Battle of Alsace under its new army commander, General Devers. On 2 January it had withdrawn to fortified positions in the French Maginot Line. Two days later it had taken the completely inexperienced Task Force Linden under command. Now, in the framework of the transfer of the Rhine front to de Lattre's First French Army, the French *3me Division d'Infanterie Algeriénne*, which was scheduled to take over from Task Force Linden, was also placed under General Wyche's command.

When higher command had sat on its thumbs for hours, General Brooks woke to the danger which the new German attack presented. He rang Wyche, who was not at all pleased with his huge front and the motley force now under his command, and told him urgently, 'Get out in there and get it cleaned up, it's got to be cleaned up pronto! We can't let them build up there!'[4]

Wyche sprang into action. He ordered the men of 42nd Division's infantry, which made up Task Force Linden, to attack astride the road from Weyersheim to Gambsheim. But although these men bore the insignia of the old Rainbow Division, which had won immortal glory in France in the First World War, they were greenhorns. Kicking off their attack at a quarter to four that Friday afternoon, they immediately became bogged down at the Landgraben Canal. Himmler's *Grenadiere* held them easily with automatic fire. After a while, however, they managed to slip across the Canal on the right flank and reach the Kleingraben Creek, between the canal and the town. But as it began to grow dark and the men on the right flank lost contact with the right, confusion and uncertainty set in. As the history of the Seventh Army puts it delicately: 'Darkness and loss of contact . . . forced a withdrawal to the west bank of the canal for reorganization.'[5]

It was the same in the other areas in which the Americans were attacking the new bridgehead. North of Kilstett men of the Task Force were held up by heavy artillery fire. Further attacks in two-battalion strength were stopped at Bischwiller and the Americans could do little more than dig in. Suddenly Wyche was no longer attacking – he was defending! And all the while the Germans were building up their bridgehead with amazing strength, putting more and more troops across on barges and makeshift bridges. By nightfall they had a bridgehead five miles long and two miles deep, with nearly two divisions of troops across. Himmler might win that coveted Knight's Cross yet. Soon a hard-pressed Wyche would be telling General

Brooks that things were not going at all well in the Gambsheim Bridgehead: 'The real trouble is this mushroom organization, plus the greenness of the troops, and the lack of communications. . . . I'm very sorry to have to present this situation, but that's the way it is.'[6]

All that Friday morning alarming messages had been reaching the headquarters of the 275th Infantry Regiment, desperately trying to hold on to Philippsbourg, or that part of it in American hands: 'Corps states enemy may attack Rothbach and Zinswiller any time now'; 'Elements of German 951st Infantry just west of Baerenthal'; Seventy vehicles, column of 17th SS Panzer Grenadier Division six miles north of Philippsbourg'; 'A lot of stuff is coming from the north.'[7]

Now it was generally anticipated that the enemy was going to mount a three-division armoured thrust from the north. Frederick, of the 45th, his corps commander Brooks, and half-a-dozen other generals were busy trying to work out what was going on; while in the battered little town itself the helpless survivors waited for orders. Surprisingly enough they were to *attack*, not to *defend*!

So the wearisome business of the previous day began once again. The attackers were to advance out of Philippsbourg and run the last of the German defenders out of town. But almost at once, as the German gunners began shelling the Americans, the attackers ran into trouble. Suddenly the tankers who were accompanying the attack became 'gun-shy'. As the Regimental Colonel, Colonel Malloy, recalled afterwards, 'A tank leader came forward in his tank to the corner where three of us were in a shed. He said he wouldn't advance.'[8]

Malloy's Irish temper flared. He whipped out his forty-five and told the unknown tank officer to move out to the attack – *or else*! That did the trick. The tank officer moved out.

Now Malloy personally took charge of the attack. He bumped into a group of frightened Americans busily engaged in 'withdrawing'. Again Malloy's temper flared. He gave them a tongue-lashing and threatened them with his pistol. They moved back into the attack. Heavy enemy fire held it up for a while, but a Lieutenant Heck, using a light machine-gun, firing it from the hip like an automatic, got the attack moving again, while Malloy exclaimed, 'Who is that crazy guy? Let's get him a medal!'

The attackers now began to find the survivors of their first failed attack who had been in hiding for a couple of days. A medical officer and a GI were brought up from a wine cellar, unshaven and starving. They told the attackers they had hidden in the back of a chicken coop at the far end of the cellar. One of them had had a very bad cold and he had to time his coughing with the cackling of the chickens. He said he had almost choked to death holding back his coughing.[9]

Now the steam was going out of the attack and Malloy had trouble with gun-shy tankers again. He came across them bickering with the weary, sweating infantrymen. They would only advance down the street, where they were sitting ducks for the Germans' deadly *panzerfausts* (a kind of bazooka), if they were accompanied by foot soldiers. Malloy gave them a direct order to advance. Reluctantly the Shermans began to roll once more. Behind them the infantry-men sheltered, crouched as if against heavy rain. Malloy went with them, in spite of the fact that he had now been wounded in the shoulder.

Suddenly a shell exploded nearby. Metal fragments hissed through the air. Malloy howled with pain and went down. He had been hit in the leg and could not walk. A sergeant and an officer helped him into the basement of the nearest house. Jack Malloy's part in the Battle of Philippsbourg was over. As soon as the tank commander saw what had happened, he reversed and disappeared down the street, leaving the infantry to their fate.

But in Philippsbourg itself the Germans' resistance was almost over. Lieutenant Brogan, who had led the attack the previous day, waited in a foxhole for the order to attack a nearby ridge. Next to him in the two-man foxhole, his platoon sergeant, Martinez, snored loudly, completely worn out. Suddenly a shell exploded nearby and Martinez woke with a start. Next to him Brogan yelled, 'I'm hit!'

With trembling hands Martinez began to cut away the officer's uniform to ascertain the extent of his injuries. Then he gasped with horror.

'As I cut away I could see this red gooey mess.'[10] Lieutenant Brogan had suffered that fate dreaded by all combat soldiers, worse than death itself. *His balls had been shot off!*

However, Martinez continued to cut 'and somehow the red, gooey stuff didn't seem like flesh and blood any more. It was too sticky, and there seemed glass fragments mixed in with it.'[11] Finally Martinez figured out what had happened. Brogan had been carrying a jar of strawberry jam in his overcoat pocket when he had been hit. The shell fragment had gone through the jar and its contents and still had enough force to nick him in the inside thigh. 'It had made a small hole but *not* the horrible one that he and I imagined,' Sergeant Martinez recalled. All the same Lieutenant Brogan was evacuated and the 70th Division lost another brave leader.

At Wingen, in spite of the new threat and the American High Command's realization that, whether they liked it or not, they would soon have to withdraw even further the 70th Division was attacking there too.

While Colonel Cheves' E and F Companies moved up to take over the attack from his G Company which had borne the brunt of the fighting so far, a strange thing happened. The weary men of George stood by, watching the new men move up. They were tired and short-tempered. They felt they had been doing all the fighting by themselves. Suddenly, as one of their NCOs recalled afterwards, 'I saw the fellow in front of me drop and hit the ground. Everybody in turn dropped just like a long row of up-ended dominoes, each domino knocking down the one behind it!'[12] They had not been hit by enemy fire. What had happened was the result of a battlefield psychosis. As the sergeant explained: 'We were all sheepish when we realized that nothing was wrong, just some guy up front with the 'willies'. Fighting makes you that way, on edge, quick-acting.'[13]

That incident seemed symbolic of the whole confused irrational mess at Wingen that Friday. Just as Cheves' other two companies moved into the attack, an American tank started to blast away at Cheves and his staff. 'As I watched, almost petrified, it let go with a broadside into the trees all around us. It was a terrible feeling to lie there hugging the ground while that monster blasted away.'[14]

Now the Colonel moved on again to see 'a platoon of American infantrymen make a most amazing attack across an open field directly in front of us, the like of which I doubt has ever been duplicated since the Revolutionary days when soldiers marched into battle keeping a straight line while the drummer boy beat away on his drum.'[15]

Suddenly the German machine guns burst into fire. Simultaneously the whole line went down. 'It was impossible to ascertain how many had been hit, for the entire line lay still, flat on their bellies while the enemy guns continued to rattle away.'[16]

That day Sergeant Richard Armstrong was a platoon guide in the 276th Infantry's A Company. Just before the company had gone into the attack, their mess sergeant had tried to feed the infantrymen a superb roast turkey dinner. But after a week on cold 'C' and 'K' rations their stomachs had shrunk so much that, to Sergeant Armstrong's disgust, he could only eat a small portion of the hot food. For many of the men it would be their last ever meal, hot or cold.

All day they had attacked, losing more and more men all the time. Now the company, what was left of it, was readied to attack yet another hill. The survivors had been told that there would be a preparatory artillery barrage on the German positions before they attacked. In due course, the 'barrage' arrived, all four rounds of it. 'Just enough to wake the Krauts up,' Armstrong said grimly.

Then they were moving forward up the hill in a slow, careful skirmish line, with bayonets fixed. Up in the lead, as scouts, were Armstrong and his friend, Dave Peirotti. They flushed out the first of the enemy. Most of them surrendered quickly. Then the German artillery opened up and Pierotti was hit. His jaw hung from his face by shreds of gory flesh. He disappeared to the rear. Another rifleman, Pfc Kufersen, advancing next to Armstrong, was hit by a German who popped up from a hole only ten yards away. Instinctively Armstrong fired from the hip and the German went down. Armstrong turned to the wounded Kufersen. 'Joe,' he told him, looking down at the ashen-faced youngster, 'you're heading back to the States.' He looked up and said weakly, 'Dick, I'm too young to die.' Armstrong never saw him again.

Armstrong's CO, Lieutenant Doegnes, known behind his back as 'Dogears', ordered him to find the Company's 2nd platoon and flank the German positions on the crest from the right. Armstrong doubled off to carry out the order, but when he reached the platoon he found that there was only one man left on his feet with a squad capable of still fighting, Sergeant Red Shelander. Together, the handful of men and the two NCOs attempted to carry out 'Dogears'' order. But by the time they had reached the crest, Armstrong and Red were the only two left; the rest had fallen in the snow behind them.

A tremendous artillery barrage now descended on the two lone noncoms. Armstrong flung himself behind two huge boulders and Red hid behind a snowbank. As the snow blackened around them and the shells stripped the branches off the pines in a shower of green rain, German infantry began to advance on the two survivors. But they were still full of fight. Armstrong kept popping up and loosing off a quick burst with his M-1 and ducking again, with the result that Red, whom the Germans could see, received all their return fire. Exasperated beyond measure, Red shouted across to his comrade during a pause in the fighting, 'Armstrong, you fire one more goddam shot, and I'll shoot you myself!'

But in the end they had to abandon their positions. They retired down the hill, finding the area 'devastated, bodies everywhere', until they found an officer, Lieutenant Arnest. He sat propped against a tree, a shrapnel wound in his stomach, hands clasping it, red with blood. He told the two NCO's 'Take the walking wounded and get the hell back to the battalion CP!'

Armstrong picked up Curly Uczunski, who had been shot in the leg, while Red selected Pfc Theo Renk, who had a 'million dollar wound'. He had been hit in the buttocks, or so they thought. Now as Arnest held off the Germans with his carbine, the two NCOs staggered off with their heavy loads through the deep snow. Within minutes they were lathered with sweat and gasping like old men. So they decided to lighten their loads. They flipped a coin and Armstrong lost. He threw away his rifle but kept his cartridge belt, while Red dropped the latter and kept his rifle. They stumbled from the scene of the disaster, passing dead and wounded GIs every few yards, the cries for help getting fainter and fainter until they vanished.

They struggled on, occasionally putting Curly down in the snow and dragging him like a sledge by his collar. All the time Theo Renk moaned that he wanted 'to take a piss'. But every time they set him up he confessed that he couldn't urinate. Soon they'd find out why. And all the while the Germans opened fire on them every time they crossed a ridge-line. Once a shell slammed into the snow close by, but it was a dud and the NCOs shook their fists at the unseen enemy gunners.

In the end they reached an aid station and delivered the two wounded men to a doctor. But it was already too late for Theo. He was dead. The doctor showed them the tiny shrapnel wound in his stomach. It had done terrible damage to his lower body – hence his inability to urinate. He had been dying all the time they had fought to bring him in. The two NCOs and six other wounded men were the only survivors of 180 men of A Company who had landed so confidently at Marseilles only four weeks before.[17]

And so it went on through a day of confused horror and purposeless slaughter. As it drew to a close, 'Big Jim' Reed of B Company started handing out rations to the weary survivors, tears streaming down his unshaven face. Finally he came to the last man in the line, Sergeant Leroy Rowley. But Jim choked, knowing that the full company numbered over a hundred, 'God, there are only thirty-eight of you left.'[18]

Colonel Cheves was similarly affected. His father had died in the First World War and he remembered his grandmother's tales of the Civil War in Virginia: 'a cannon ball down the chimney and dead soldiers on the porch'. His sergeant from the aid station came in to report the day's casualties: 'There's a lot of men getting hurt up there, Colonel,' he said. 'Four killed and twenty-four wounded, most of them in George Company.'

'The cold figures depressed me, for I hadn't realized that so many had been hit. I didn't dare say anything for a few seconds as I stood there, staring at the light in the far corner. It all seemed like a dream.'

But now his sadness turned into a burning anger. 'I know it,' he snorted to the medic, 'and a lot of them could have been prevented if there hadn't been so damn much confusion up there. I've never seen so much mess in all my life. Nobody knows what they're doing!'[19]

Now it was to be the turn of the French. On that afternoon of Friday, 5 January, as de Lattre's First Army prepared to withstand the expected German attack out of the Colmar Pocket and, further north, to take their part in the Allied attack into the new Gambsheim Bridgehead, the American Inspector-General of the Sixth Army Group reported to SHAEF on the state of a typical French formation: 'It is not in a condition to be used in an offensive role until it has received suitable equipment and has been trained for a period of *not less than four months!*'[20] In spite of de Gaulle's bold words to Eisenhower at the 3 January conference, de Lattre knew just how true the unknown Inspector-General's report on his army was. Even as he prepared to fight, the hook-nosed Army Commander, running his force from the comfort of the Hotel de la Balance in the town of Montbeliard, well away from the fighting, knew that his First Army was heading for a crisis.

'King Jean', at the age of 55, was at the height of his career in January, 1945. At last he had achieved the dream of every regular army officer: he commanded a whole army. 'King Jean' made the most of it, too. He loved glittering uniforms, decorations, parades and ceremonies and thought nothing of making his soldiers wait for hours for his appearance on the parade ground. If he wanted something in the middle of the night – a drink, an aspirin (for he was often ill) – he would not hesitate to ring for his orderly although the object needed might well be on his bedside table. He was a terrible stickler for discipline and correct appearance; and it was said that his hawklike gaze, just like Napoleon's, could strip a man naked, physically and mentally.

In 1940 he had been a mere colonel, chief-of-staff in the armoured division commanded by de Gaulle. But unlike his chief, he had not gone into exile at the defeat of France. Instead he had sworn an oath of loyalty to Marshal Pétain and had tamely served for two long years as a divisional commander in Unoccupied France, while elsewhere total war raged. In November, 1942, however, when the Germans had marched into Unoccupied France as a result of the Allied invasion of French North Africa, he had been the only senior officer in Pétain's army to offer them resistance. He had subsequently been arrested by the French authorities, but had escaped to England by submarine. From there he had made his way to General de Gaulle and offered to join the Free French Army in the fight against the Boche. There, in Algiers, it was said, de Gaulle had greeted him with 'You haven't changed.'

His one-time Chief-of-Staff grinned, accepting the proffered hand, and replied, 'You've got bigger'.[21]

Thereafter, following two years of inactivity, de Lattre's career had taken off. In Italy he had fought as a corps commander with distinction. In August, 1944, he had been given command of the First French Army for the invasion of Southern France, where he would lead it successfully for four months until finally the Germans stopped him at Colmar. Typical of 'King Jean' was the order he had given to his generals on the eve of that Southern France invasion. He had told them, 'Whatever you do, don't crush the vines!'[22]

But over the long months of fighting (even years in the case of those who had supported de Gaulle from the first) his men had become demoralized, feeling that they had been abandoned by the bulk of the French people. At the beginning of the Ardennes offensive, de Lattre had written to de Gaulle: 'Among all ranks, but particularly among the officers, even at a high level, there is a general impression that the nation is ignoring them and deserting them. The basic cause of this malaise rests in the apparent non-participation of the country in the war'.[23]

De Lattre was right, of course. The French wanted to get on with living again, just as they had done back in 1939, or even up to June, 1944. Most of them had led a good life prior to the Allied invasion, especially those who lived on the land. All that Paris saw of the war now was the US black market between the Opera and the Madeleine and the drunken GIs with their whores in 'Pig Alley.'

For most French civilians, the soldiers of de Lattre's army were playing games there in Alsace, doing nothing but guard a lot of crazy Boches in the Colmar Pocket. So the men of the First felt themselves as much divorced from their country as did the GIs whose homes were three thousand miles away across the Atlantic.

Now this demoralized army, ill-equipped with obsolete Allied cast-offs, was to face an all-out attack by the best army in the world. That day de Lattre seemed to realize that he could not hold the line against the Boche unless he received American aid. More, he needed the moral support of the surety that the Americans would not retreat in the north. Plagued by doubts and fears, de Lattre made the journey to Devers' headquarters at Vittel.

'Our conversation at once took a lively and frank turn,' he wrote after the war. 'The man was direct, but this realist hid a sensitive nature under a sometimes rough exterior. We passed events in review; then I told him of my preoccupations, reminding him that he was himself the grandson of an Alsatian woman. Much moved, he assured me that, despite the risks, the US 6th Army Corps would cover the left flank of the 1st Army and would fight on the Maginot Line.'[24]

Although de Lattre had Devers' promise, there was still the question of Strasbourg. On the whole length of the Rhine above the Alsatian capital there were only a handful of troops, American and French. But such considerations did not seem to bother de Lattre at this moment of crisis. He ordered his dashing Gascon corps commander, General de Monsabert, who three years before had been fighting American troops in North Africa to 'defend Strasbourg at any price!'[25]

One consideration, however, which seems to have escaped de Lattre as he ordered the last ditch stand in the face of imminent German attack was: if de Monsabert, bold and gallant as he was, failed to hold the Germans to the south of the capital, where were the troops to come from to defend Strasbourg? The manpower barrel in the Allied camp was scraped clean.

TWO

De Lattre's counter-attack into the Gambsheim bridgehead failed almost at once. The plan was for the American 314th Infantry Regiment to attack Drusenheim and Herrlisheim on the northern flank of the bridgehead, while the French attacked Kilstett on the southern flank. The Americans kicked off first. For a while they met with limited success, but soon their luck ran out. A savage counter-attack, carried out with the usual German verve, hit the advancing American infantry and put an end to their attack. The Americans either withdrew or dug in.

Then the French started their advance with infantry led by tanks. Almost immediately the tanks ran into the German anti-tank screen. Several batteries of 57mm anti-tank guns were dug in in the woods which bordered the Rhine. In quick succession, as the solid white blurs of anti-tank shells zipped across the fields, tank after tank reeled to a halt, flames spurting from the stalled Shermans. The French armoured attack came to a rapid halt.

Still the infantry persisted. Led by a battalion of the Foreign Legion, for de Lattre believed in bolstering up the mood of his weary soldiers with what he called 'shock battalions' of marines, paras and legionnaires, they pushed home their attack. Despite losses, the French succeeded in reaching Bettenhoffen on the southern quarter of Gambsheim. The Germans counterattacked. Grimly the men of the desert, half-a-dozen nationalities fighting under the French flag, held on under increasing German pressure. But by nightfall the legionnaires could hold on no longer. They fell back with serious losssses. The French First Army's clash with the Germans had been a total failure.

Meanwhile, the Americans were doing little better. Once more Task

Force Linden attempted to storm Gambsheim and throw the Germans back into the Rhine from whence they had come. They pressed ever closer to the picturesque riverside village with its half-timbered houses and storks' nests on the red-tiled roofs. But the Germans were not going to give up their precious bridgehead. The senior German officers knew and feared Himmler's wrath. They threw the Americans back and in the end the men of the once-famed Rainbow Division gave up for the day.

That evening General Wyche called Corps Commander Brooks and told him he thought Task Force Linden's chances of ever taking the place were very slim. 'They've been *in* and *out* twice,' he said grimly to his Corps Commander and drew the latter's attention to the fact that the Rainbow Division's men had suffered heavy casualties due to 'their state of training, organization, and operation etc'.[1]

In fact, he said, they had been put in the line in what was supposedly a quiet sector to make up for their lack of proper training. Now the Rainbow men found themselves right in the centre of the action.

But General Wyche had other things to worry about besides the deficiencies of the untrained Rainbow Division that Saturday morning. A new threat had loomed up, which was directly affecting his own 79th Infantry. Two experienced armoured divisions, the 21st and 25th Panzer, supported by the paras of the German Seventh Parachute Division, were now breaking out in the north in a new threat, obviously intent on capturing the key town of Haguenau. There, it was clear, they would link up with the Germans attacking out of the Gambsheim bridgehead, and if they did, it would be a disaster for General Brooks' Sixth Corps!

Now the 79th and elements of the 14th Armored Division prepared for the attack to come, as the tanks of the German strike force nosed their way down the snowbound trails in the no-man's-land between themselves and the Americans. Cooks arid clerks – anyone who could be pressed into service – went up front and worked feverishly and without rest to improve their defensive positions. Hasty minefields were laid, concertina wire strung out, trees felled to block trails, booby traps set up, as the afternoon wore on.

The GIs could hear the rattle of tracks to their front, the roar of tank engines labouring up gradients, the sharp angry bursts of machine-gun fire, whether friendly or enemy nobody knew. Tension was in the air. The infantry knew from bitter experience how one single Panzer could roll up a whole company. The tankers, for their part, knew just how ineffective their own tanks were against the mighty Tigers and Panthers. Their Shermans were underarmoured and outgunned. A Tiger could knock out a Sherman at a range of nearly a mile. A Sherman, however, would have to get within three hundred yards even to have a chance of knocking out an enemy tank!

The noise grew louder. There was the sound of snapping trees. Cries in German could be heard as their infantry advanced with the tanks. Then there they were, a line of infantry coming out of the gloom, supported by ten tanks, sixty-ton monsters, which nothing could stop! The GIs of the 79th's 313th Regiment opened fire from their outposts of Aschbach and Stundwiller. But there was no stopping the attackers. They surged forward with the old elan, as if these were the great days of 1940 when nothing had been able to hold up the victorious *Grossdeutsche Wehrmacht*. Fighting desperately, the men of the 79th were forced to pull back. A platoon was cut off. Desperately it fought its way back, leaving the snow behind it littered with dead and dying.

The Germans hit the main line of the 3rd Battalion, 313th Regiment. Fifteen tanks rumbled into the attack. The first one hit the hastily planted mines. It rattled to a stop, its left track trailing behind it. A moment later another disappeared in a flash of blinding light. Now the defenders' anti-tank guns opened up. Another and another German tank shuddered to a halt, gleaming silver scars suddenly appearing on their grey metal hides. Suddenly the steam went out of the German attack and the survivors started to withdraw, the enemy infantry falling back, leaving their dead and dying behind them. For the time being the 'Cross of Lorraine' Division men had held the enemy, but soon they would be back. For here was soon to begin what General Devers would later describe as 'one of the greatest defensive battles in Europe in World War Two.'

Indeed, on the whole length of General Devers' long front the only successes the Sixth Army Group could record after a whole week's bitter fighting were in the hotly contested villages of Philippsbourg and Wingen. At the former the Germans attempted a counterattack at four in the morning. A Pfc Saeger of the 70th Division spotted the infiltrators sneaking out of the woods. 'German patrol,' he hissed to his men. His section dropped as one. For his part Seager hid behind a wood pile, but a German spotted him there and told him to put up his hands. Seager pressed the trigger of his weapon and the German fell, as if poleaxed, three slugs stitched across his stomach. Seager recorded, 'He started groaning louder than hell and then the rest of the Heinies tossed a hand grenade. It landed on his prone body. I didn't hear a whimper after that.'[2]

With that heady confidence that all new units feel once they have had their first taste of action and before they become jaded and fearful, the men of the 70th now went into the attack. They rushed what they called '88 Corner', hit a road block, and had overwhelmed the Germans before they knew what was happening. They started climbing the hill beyond, but, as Sergeant Links remembered afterwards, 'There were Jerries on the hill and we soon walked right into them. They opened up and the fight was on. We gained the upper hand and kept on going. . . . The Jerries ran for their holes as we closed in.'[3]

The Germans rallied and counterattacked. A hand-to-hand struggle developed. A German appeared to be surrendering, hands raised. He had just thrown a grenade which had killed two of the attackers. Now the men of the 70th made as if they were going to shoot him. His face contorted with fear, the German pleaded, '*Nein, nein, ich habe Frau und Kinder!*'

At the last moment, the Americans let him go. But now their blood was up, carried away by the crazy death-wish of battle. Another prisoner appeared. Sergeant Kelsey of the 70th raised his rifle. He was going to shoot the German. Impassively the prisoner waited for the end, but the rifle refused to fire. In his rage, Kelsey ripped out the magazine and flung it at the bemused German!

At Wingen things were also going well for the Americans. Young Private Hy Schorr, a machine-gunner from New York, going into action with the 274th Infantry of the 70th Division, had just spent the night in a foxhole with his buddy bleeding to death next to him. Now he advanced with the rest of his company, seeing 'houses aflame and the surrounding countryside well lit'. He passed a 'dead German identifiable by his coal-scuttle helmet. Both arms were straight up in the air. He was frozen stiff!'[4]

The attackers pressed on. Below, Wingen seemed remarkably quiet, perhaps too quiet. Had the Germans gone?

They hadn't. As they approached the first houses, the slits in their basements started spitting fire. It was a furious and bloody fight at close range. The Krauts battled desperately and refused to give up, while the men of Fox Company continued to pour in the grenades. Pfc Soper was hit and fell right by one of the windows.

Brush, the medic, moved calmly to where Soper lay. Four shots passed between Brush's legs, knocking the bayonet off the rifle of a man nearby. Soper kept yelling, "Get the rats out of their hole . . . get'em boys." Sgt Renzaglia yelled, "Watch out, Soper, we're going to throw some grenades." Hearing this, Soper used his one good arm and grabbed a grenade from under his shirt, pulled the pin with his teeth, and threw it through the window.

A loud explosion followed, and then a surviving rifleman stuck his rifle out the window, against Soper's chest and fired twice. Dieckman grabbed a German medic and shouted for him to get inside and tell the remainder that a tank was coming up to "blast all hell out of them."

There was no tank, but the dodge worked. The final eleven Germans ran out, yelling 'Kamerad' and surrendered. But Soper was dead. Another leader had fallen in the attack.

The mood of the attacking Americans was becoming savage and the Germans had to surrender swiftly if they wanted to live. Sergeant R. Armstrong of A Company, whose first experience of combat the day before had been the sight of a major running wildly through the woods, waving his .45 and yelling, 'Take to the hills, men, the Germans are coming!', now found himself lodged in a ruined house observing the unsuspecting Germans. A little earlier a burst of enemy fire had shot one of their medics, 'Doc' Moore, who had gone out to help a wounded infantryman. He raised his rifle and fired eight shots at the Germans *and missed each time*!

'Hey,' he yelled to Platoon Sergeant Bob Brewer, 'I've spotted the bastards who shot Doc.'

Brewer shouted back, 'Move aside boy and I'll show you how to do it.' The platoon sergeant waited patiently for two of the Germans to reappear and then shot them both.

A German medic came out into the road beyond the church waving a Red Cross flag. Armstrong raised his rifle. Brewer put his hand on his colleague's shoulder. 'Don't shoot, Dick,' he hissed. 'Wait till he gets a little closer. Then you can't miss.'

A little later Armstrong saw another German zig-zagging down the street. He felt that the 'Kraut should at least be scared', so he glanced down the rifle barrel and 'touched one off'.[5] To Armstrong's amazement, the German dropped dead next to the medic and his platoon cheered.

The killing of the German and American medics was typical. The battle had been too fierce, too intent, too murderous for either side to care about the niceties of conduct and the Rules of Land Warfare. Little quarter was given or expected.

Following up the first attack, the new boy, Hy Schorr, burdened with his machine gun and boxes of ammunition, noted the trail of destruction his comrades had left in their wake, the pathetic pieces of flotsam and jetsam which had once been men. 'I saw a GI lying flat on his back,' Schorr recalled. 'Someone had evidently tried first aid, for bandages were tied loosely around his head. Strewn about him, too, were V-mail letters and other personal items. We stopped behind a knocked-out American half-track. Inside were six dead Germans, some of them with their feet dangling over the side. We followed the route which Fox Company had attacked that morning. Here was a sight I would not forget. We trudged slowly by and the sight sickened us to complete silence. In the ditches on both sides of the road were numerous bodies, all of them American. They lay frozen as they had fallen.'[6]

Schorr set up his position in a two-storey house ready to cover the next stage of the advance and again he encountered nothing but horror. As he set his gun up on a table, he didn't notice at first, 'but under the table was the half-naked body of a German soldier. He was a blond young fellow and good-looking. Around his bare chest was a strip of cloth used as a bandage. He had been severely wounded and died right there. No one seemed inclined to remove him. In fact, his body served as a brace to keep the table from moving. There were at least another dozen dead Germans in the house. In the next room lay an enormous Kraut, his body whitened with fallen plaster and half covered with debris. The smell of death was all through the house.'[7]

Still the killing went on in Wingen. Heavy firing from the direction of the cemetery was now holding up the advance. Lieutenant James Haines decided to make a dash for it. He shouted back to his senior NCO, Sergeant Petty, 'Pass the word back to break out one at a time through the door.' He gripped his carbine. 'I'm going *now*!'

He pelted across the street, pursued by bullets, but he made it. Another man followed, and another. Haines began to think the whole platoon would make it, but that wasn't to be. One of his platoon named Goode had just started his dash for safety when there was a burst of machine-gun fire. Goode tottered and fell back into a ditch.[8]

Casualties were now mounting steadily. In Colonel Cheves' Fox Company half its complement of 120 men had been killed or wounded in the first three hours of the attack. Now Cheves heard that Lieutenant Mahon, commanding the Company, had just been killed. It gave Cheves a cold feeling to think Mahon was dead. A wife and two children awaited his return. Then he heard that Pfc Morningstar, the radio operator, had just been killed too.

'Who is in command of your company now?' he asked the messenger who brought the news.

'I don't know, sir.'

'Do you have many men with you?'

'No, sir. Most of my platoon have been hit, sir.'[9]

Cheves threw in his G and E companies. At dusk the surviving SS men launched a fanatical counterattack into the flanks of G Company. Sergeant Kirk of G Company said afterwards, 'It was almost dark and fires from burning buildings furnished an eerie light as we went to work setting up a defense, evacuating the wounded and herding prisoners to the rear. Suddenly all hell broke loose! There was the chattering of machine guns, followed by terrific explosions, one after another, jarring the buildings and sprinkling broken glass. Through the noises a voice screamed, "*I can't see. I can't see!*"'

The voice died away. Almost immediately another shell exploded nearby. Sergeant Wilmoth dashed by, headed towards the rear with blood streaming down his side. Pfc Kliever let out a blood-curdling yell and his bloody arm dangled by his side. 'God, it was awful!'[10]

The Germans came running down the street 'whooping like a bunch of Red Indians'. In an instant all was confusion. Bazookas fired. Hand grenades were tossed back and forth. An American machine gun opened up, slow and sedate, unlike the high-pitched hysterical hiss of the German MG 42 which could fire 1,000 rounds per minute. But it did the job all the same. The German line faltered. Next moment the SS were running back the way they had come, leaving their dead and dying behind.

The end was near for the SS now. During their week of combat in the West, the two battalions employed in the battle of Wingen had lost 650 men out of the original 900. As Lieutenant Zoepf recalled: 'Both sides were exhausted. A lull ensued and during this temporary lull, the 1st and 3rd Battalions started to disengage their units carefully from the enemy.'[11] Distributing the last of their ammunition among the survivors, releasing their 400 enlisted men prisoners, but taking ten officer prisoners with them, the SS set off into the woods through which they had come in what now seemed another age.

With the aid of a captured American map, Zoepf led the way for what was left of his decimated battalion. But this time the 22-year-old veteran was not destined to escape. Quite soon they ran into a tank, almost buried in the snow. Someone tossed a grenade into its open turret and it started to burn at once. Nearby dug-in American infantry opened up and Zoepf was hit in the leg.

The SS scattered in confusion and Zoepf found himself struggling on alone. He stumbled across a foxhole. At first he thought it was empty, but then a GI appeared. While Zoepf stared transfixed, the GI raised his rifle and fired. At ten yards' range he missed! Later Zoepf discovered that he had lost his glasses and was as blind as a bat. He didn't give him a second chance. Hobbling forward, he slammed his clenched fist down on the GI's helmet, knocking him to the bottom of the hole, just as American mortars opened up close by. While the bombs howled down all around, Zoepf knelt on his terrified prisoner, his Walther pistol in his hand. His wounded leg started to stiffen. He stretched it out, to encounter something soft! Cowering next to his first prisoner there was another GI alive and very frightened! Time passed slowly. Once he heard shouts in German. He waved his ski cap furiously. But the SS crept by without noticing him. He tried his school English on his two prisoners, who were no longer so frightened. One of them was from Texas. He offered to bandage Zoepf's wounded leg. In return the German offered them looted US cigarettes.

Now, as the first light of dawn filtered through the trees, Zoepf found himself in the middle of a dug-in American company. About this time a sergeant came across and ordered the man without glasses to help collect the dead. Under cover of a GI blanket, Zoepf pressed his pistol into the helpless American's back and told him to find a good excuse for not going away. The GI began to sweat and said he was not feeling so well, which was quite true. The sergeant bought the excuse the first time, but not the second. He came across and snarled, 'If you crazy sonovabitches are too lazy to get up, then gimme ya blanket!' He reached down and snatched it away angrily *to reveal Zoepf!*

For one moment there was total silence. The sergeant stared down at the SS officer and Zoepf stared back. Then the SS officer tossed away his pistol and pandemonium broke out. Immediately he was surrounded by GIs, clamouring for souvenirs. His black leather coat, his decorations, his shoulder patches were ripped off and only at the very last moment were the souvenir hunters stopped from snatching away his wedding ring. Zoepf's war was over.

For the 400 prisoners of the Germans in Wingen it was all over too. 250 of them were locked up in the Catholic church, which had been strongly defended the previous day. Now Sergeant Dyes and PFC Dubose of the 70th Division approached the building cautiously, grenades in their hands, ready to toss them in through a shattered window. Suddenly the door swung open and a horde of Americans rushed out. All of them had one single question on their lips: '*Where's the rear?*' And that's the direction in which they headed immediately they were told!

At the next village, Zittersheim, there was a tremendous reunion celebration as old buddies of the 45th Division spotted each other, hugging one another and clapping each other's backs, tears streaming down their faces. One of them was Ben Stein, free at last. He remembers sharing K-rations and water. 'It never tasted better!'[12]

General Herren, the commander of the 70th Division, was also interested in the prisoners. He asked Colonel Cheves in Wingen, 'How many have you rescued so far?'

Cheves replied, 'Approximately one hundred and fifty.'

Herren then asked, 'Did you find any Germans dressed in American uniforms?'

Cheves said he had a man checking on it, and then, wanting to get rid of the General, who of late had always seemed to be cluttering up *his* battlefield, he suggested Herren should take shelter in a large foxhole nearby, which he did. Now Cheves left him and watched his excited, unshaven men enjoying the fruits of their victory. One of them had found a quart of Schenley's and was passing it round among his buddies, who were taking great swigs straight from the bottle. An army photographer came up to record the victory and took pictures of men breaking down doors with their rifle butts. The usual exhibitionist, always found on such occasions, had his photograph taken, riding around on a rickety old bicycle, wearing a looted top hat. But there were sad moments, too. Hy Schorr, the machine-gunner, remembers, 'It was snowing heavily when I stepped outside. There were several dead German soldiers scattered around and I noticed a GI from another outfit examining the bodies very closely. I hesitated to approach him, but finally touched his shoulder.

'"What are you looking for?" I asked.

He looked at me. '"Are you Graves Registration?"'[13]

Schorr learned that the man had a brother-in-law in Fox Company who had been reported missing in action. Now he took every opportunity to dig bodies out of the snow to look for him. Schorr left him searching in the snow. In fact, the brother-in-law had been dead nearly two days.

Colonel Cheves felt sad and depressed in spite of his victory. He allowed the army camera man to take his photo, pointing to the smoking village in the background and 'felt like a heel. I was no hero and I had not taken the town. The real heroes who had done the job were my men who had slugged it out toe to toe with the best soldiers in Hitler's Army and had won.'[14]

He left the photographer and wandered through the village. His men seemed 'so tired and there was an apathetic expression on their faces'.[15] But the dead soldiers affected him most. 'I had to choke back my feelings when I saw them lying dead in the streets and ditches. There were dead everywhere, men I knew, stretched out on the cold ground, surrounded by Germans, frozen into fantastic positions. Everywhere I looked, in the middle of the streets, in the ditches, in the buildings, on the embankments, on steps, everywhere there were dead frozen soldiers. I never again saw so many dead together in one small area. It seemed such a shame, and it was hard to realize that they were actually dead, especially the ones I had known, the ones I had talked with a day or so before. War had always seemed so useless to me, and now it seemed even more repugnantly futile.'[16]

General Jacob Devers had had his first victory, however small, in this first week of the battle of Alsace. But the price had been high. In Philippsbourg alone the 275th Infantry Regiment had suffered over 1,000 casualties; just short of one third of its total strength the day it had gone into the line. The butcher's bill was indeed high, and as always it was the young who paid it.

The Battle of Wingen was over, too, and the survivors started their painful trudge up the heights away from the battered town back to where they had started in what now seemed another age.

They had been promised a rest, but it never came. As the weary men plodded by him, Colonel Cheves received new orders for his battalion. They read: 'Assemble your men in Puberg (a nearby village from whence they had started their attack). Trucks will arrive there. Proceed to Oberbronn, arriving there before daylight tomorrow.'

Engineers prepare holes for TNT charges on a road near Philippsbourg, December, 1944.

Engineers, pressed into service as infantrymen, watch from an attic window.

General Herren, commander of the 70th Division.

American troops man a 57 mm anti-tank gun near Reipertswiller, January, 1945.

A moment of relaxation for American troops of the 70th Division.

Gun crew of 79th Division trying to keep warm, Alsace, January, 1945.

A mortar crew prepares a barrage of white phosphorus shells.

A French woman and her children prepare to leave Haguenau prior to the planned withdrawal of the 7th US Army.

Civilians retreat from the battle zone with what little they can save.

An M4 tank passes through Wingen.

Men of 45th Division hunt for a sniper in the recently taken village of Niederbronn.

Wounded infantrymen of the 70th Division shelter in a protective trench near Heideneck.

Captured German soldiers under escort carry their wounded on litters.

*Wingen at the height of the battle: the town was lost and retaken
twice, in the course of which the Americans lost about 2000 men.*

A sniper's nest is knocked out.

Stretcher bearers carry wounded infantrymen away from the battle.

*Lt Edwyn Cookes shows how he feigned death behind the enemy lines
for eighteen hours. The bodies in the background are genuine casualties.*

General Alexander Patch, Commander of
US 7th Army.

"King Jean" – General de Lattre de
Tassigny, Commander of French 1st Army.

General Leclerc, Commander of 2nd French Armoured Division. He is
seen here in Germany with captured Frenchmen from the SS Division
Charlemagne. A few minutes after this photograph was taken, he had
the renegades shot.

General de Gaulle at Bayeux, Summer, 1944.

*General Robert Young, in the War Room at Ribeauville, briefs
General de Gaulle on the situation in the Colmar Pocket.*

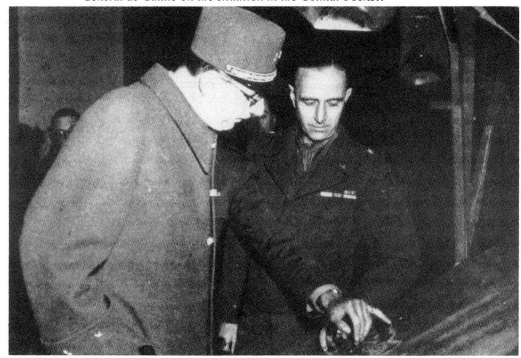

French and American troops planning a counterattack.

Nuns watch men of the US 28th Infantry Division in Rouffach.

German refugees from the fighting in Alsace sought shelter in disused mines.

Officers of the 7th Army plan the next stage of their advance from Sarreguemines.

Men of the US 12th Armoured Division on top of a camouflaged medium tank south of Colmar.

A French farmer puts flowers on the body of an American soldier.

This picture, which bears no caption, nevertheless gives some idea of what conditions were like in Alsace in the winter of 1944/45.

Across the Rhine: a white flag hangs above the ruins of a German town, March, 1945.

To an exhausted, sick Colonel Cheves, the order 'didn't seem possible, but it was. And so that night we were on the road again.'[17]

The survivors of the 70th Division were needed elsewhere and on the horizon the sky flickered the ominous pink of a fire fight. The battle went on.

THREE

It was Sunday again. Strangely enough on the northern sector of the three-pronged German attack into Alsace from north, south, and east, the front remained relatively calm, as if the Germans were exhausted by the week-long battle.

Emboldened by the lack of enemy activity, the Catholic chaplain of the 70th Division, Father McPhelin, decided he would go up front and say Mass for the survivors. Gently it was explained to him when he arrived at the CP of the Division's Second Battalion of the 275th Regiment that the war did not stop, even for God. The Battalion simply could not afford to draw men out of their foxholes for a service. It couldn't be done.

Unabashed, Father McPhelin replied, 'Well, if that's the case, I will have to go to them. That's my job.'

Half an hour later the priest was to be seen crawling on his hands and knees through the snow from foxhole to foxhole, his pockets filled with communion wafers, reminding each man that God was watching over him, encouraging them with the hackneyed phrase that begins, 'No sparrow falls from heaven without . . .'

Not all were enthused. Pfc Becker, who later reported the sudden appearance of the priest, called out mockingly as the Father crept towards his squad's sector of the front, 'You're wasting your time around here, Mike. Nobody but Protestant heathens in this company!'[1]

But Father McPhelin blessed 'the Protestant heathens' too, and crept on, searching for more Catholics. All the while the Germans, who were dug in only a hundred yards away, did not fire one single shot. 'Perhaps,' the 70th's *Divisional History* records, 'they realized what was going on and held their fire for their own spiritual reasons or out of respect for a brave man.'²

In fact, that Sunday the Germans had other problems besides the portly priest wandering around the front line distributing communion wafers. The two assault divisions in the northern sector were exhausted. The High Command had given them permission to withdraw to more favourable positions where they would be filled out with replacements prior to starting another all-out attack which would finally break the enemy resistance. Behind them they left a thin skirmish line of snipers and machine-gunners, given what the German *landser* called in his own slang *ein Himmelfahrtskommando* (an Ascension Day Commando) that is, a one-way ticket to heaven.

But the GIs didn't know that. After a couple of the 70th men had been killed by snipers that morning, men ordered to go out on patrol were distinctly jittery. As Sergeant Slater rounded up his squad for one such patrol, 'one of my men shot himself in the leg right after I woke him up. The blast nearly tore off his legs.'³ Not far away another sergeant, alerted to take out a similar patrol, simply sprayed his feet with a burst from his grease gun and that was the end of his 'fighting career'. Even senior officers were shaky and not inclined to accept orders without question. One company, ordered out to 'pretty up the line', as they saw it, was told by another company commander, 'If this were my company, I wouldn't move it a damn step until after rations arrive!'

Colonel Adams, Deputy Divisional Commander of the 45th Division, rounded on Colonel McAleer of the 70th, 'There is something we must get straightened out. This morning C Company moved out for Hill 471. At 1000 when I was at the battalion command post everyone told me that C Company was in contact with A Company. Now I'm notified that they don't know whether C Company is in position or not. They are out of contact! God damn it, man, this business of sending out a company and losing contact and forgetting all about it has got to stop. This is an order. *We've got to put the heat on these birds to do things!*'⁴

Even soldiers in comparatively safe jobs were decidedly shaky. Colonel Cheves, for instance, found that his own driver, Green, had had second thoughts about further combat. As they drove through the snowbound forest that morning, Green broke the heavy silence and asked, 'Are we going back up there where we were yesterday, Colonel?'

Cheves answered in the affirmative.

His driver pulled a face and said finally, 'I've been having a lot of pains lately and I don't know whether I can go through all that excitement again or not.'

Cheves lost his temper. 'Forget your damn pains. We've got work to do!'[5]

The unexpected lull in the fighting that second Sunday, due to the regrouping of the two German assault divisions, meant salvation for two hard-pressed Americans cut off behind enemy lines. For eighteen hours Edwin Cooke and Lieutenant Peebles had been feigning death in a ditch after their company had been virtually wiped out the day before.

Cooke had a terrible cold and, as he told his rescuers later that Sunday, 'It took a tremendous effort to suppress the coughs which seemed determined to come. I muffled my face as much as possible with my collar but some of the steam from my breath still escaped. To me, it looked like a cloud that would give me away for sure!'[6]

It didn't. Twice they were looted, but still the Germans took them for dead. Finally, however, they heard the sound of American voices and someone crying, 'Let's go!' They were saved. Minutes later, they were being fed crackers and cheese, the first food they had eaten in twenty hours.

But if everything was relatively quiet on the northern sector, another front had flared up that Sunday to the south. At dawn, as the French First Army regrouped to await the expected German attack out of the Colmar Pocket, the Germans came.

'The shock was a violent one,' General de Lattre wrote afterwards. 'In the icy dawn, over a snow-covered plain peppered with the blackish circles of shell bursts, shadowy figures advanced: huge forms of white-painted tanks and the innumerable shadows of white-shrouded infantrymen. Between the Rhône-Rhine Canal and the arms of the River Ill, two great columns moved forward.'[7]

Himmler had launched the second stage of the Upper Rhine Command's attack. On the right, nearest to the Canal, the armour of *Feldherrnhalle* Brigade was lumbering forward. Further left, toward the River Ill, the infantry of the 198th German Infantry Division in their white snowsuits, were slogging northwards. Their objective was obvious. They were heading straight for Strasbourg, the city upon which depended the fate of de Gaulle's France, perhaps even the future of the Allied coalition.

All along the line the French, with their ancient tanks, were forced to withdraw as the Germans pressed home their attack. One after another the small villages which the French had occupied, preferring the comfort of the inns to the freezing cold of foxholes, were abandoned. By noon the Germans had crossed the River Ill and had attempted to reach the main road from Sélestat to Strasbourg, but were forced back. Hurriedly the Germans tried another tack, crossing the Rhône-Rhine Canal on the only bridge which the French had failed to destroy near the village of Erstein. They rolled on. Just in time French engineers managed to blow up the last bridge before Strasbourg, thus stopping their drive less than ten miles from the city.

'As long as there's a war on and as long as there's a Third Division, the Third Division will be in that war,' the men who wore the blue-and-white patch would say. As the *Divisional History* of the Third Division commented, 'Variations on this same theme were repeated many times by the men. . . . The knowledge was omnipresent. The thought was conveyed in various shades of tone – cynically, bitterly, disgustedly . . . or confidently, resignedly, cockily . . . or in any combination.'[8]

As the German pressure began to mount on the veteran Division's long line in the south, which stretched for fifteen miles between Chatenois (west of Sélestat) and Orbey, south of La Poutroie, the Third went into action again in a vain attempt to stop the new thrust which seemed set to capture Strasbourg. As darkness fell that Sunday, the Third kicked off its new battle which would last more than a month and gain it new glory, and many more dead. Supported by tanks, two companies of infantry assaulted two tactically important hill-tops, now held by the Germans, near the village of Ribeauville. For forty-five minutes the men of the Third plodded through heavy new snow until they reached the base of the hills. There they dropped their heavy equipment and prepared for the assault. Almost immediately the defenders spotted them. Red and green signal flares hissed into the night sky, colouring the snow below a lurid hue, against which the attackers were silhouetted a stark black.

The Germans opened fire. Those terrible multiple flak wagons burst into life. They poured a steady hail of 20mm shells at the advancing Americans who appeared to be walking into a solid wall of white fire. Men went down everywhere, but the veterans struggled on. For they were General 'Iron Mike' O'Daniel's boys, who never failed to take their objective. But in the end the intense German fire from the hill-top positions proved too much even for the men of the Third. The steam went out of their attack. Men started to go to ground. Their officers and NCOs rallied them with threats and kicks and they attacked a second time. But it was no good. They simply could not reach those hill-tops. They began to dig in as best they could, all save one man: Staff Sergeant Russell Dunham, known to his buddies as 'The Arsenal'.

'The Arsenal' had gained his name from the amazing amount of lethal hardware he always lugged about with him: a dozen hand grenades hung from his suspenders, buttonholes and belt; and he had eleven full magazines of carbine ammunition stowed away all over his big body. For some, the amount of lead that 'the Arsenal' always carried on his person had been a source of humour; now he was going to show them the use he would put it to.

Ignoring the flying wall of shells above his head, he started to edge his way towards the first enemy position – a machine-gun post, hidden by heavy logs, covered with snow. Somehow or other he managed to get within ten yards of it without being spotted. Then he was on his feet, running for all he was worth, firing his carbine from the hip and flinging grenades to his front, yelling his head off like a madman.

To his front a German MG 42 machine gun burst into life. Arsenal yelled with pain and fell, a great ten-inch gash slashed across his back. Rolling madly in a slither of snow, arms and legs flailing wildly, he fell fifteen feet down the hillside. Moments later he was up again, charging from a different direction, his uniform soaked with blood. A German grenade fell at his feet, but he didn't hesitate. He knew one single second of indecision and he would be blown to bits. He aimed a mighty kick at the deadly grenade. It sailed into the air to land yards away, where it exploded harmlessly. He drew in a deep breath. Ignoring the pain in his back, he went in for the kill. The German machine-gun team loomed up in front of him. He blasted away with his carbine. The gunner and the loader fell dead. Suddenly he heard a click. His carbine was empty. Undaunted, he reached forward and dragged the third German out of the machine-gun pit. He headed for the second German machine-gun post, seventy-five yards away, leaving a crimson trail in the snow as he crawled closer. Rifle fire and exploding German grenades raked his path. Undeterred, he crawled on, ducking every now and again, as yet another grenade burst close by. Now he was in throwing distance himself. He raised his arm and lobbed the first grenade to his front. It missed the German machine gun by yards. Dunham heaved again. This time it was a bull's eye. The German machine gun disappeared in a burst of flame. Two Germans popped up from a foxhole nearby. They raised their rifles to fire at the lone American. Badly wounded as he was, Dunham was quicker. He fired a quick burst. One German fell dead. The other dropped, groaning, to the snow. The remaining German had had enough. Nothing seemed to be able to stop this one-man army. The German flung away his rifle and fled. Dunham brought him down before he had gone ten yards.

Still he had not had enough. He led his squad in another crazy attack. He knocked out a machine gun and was fired at point blank. The German missed. Dunham didn't give him a second chance. He felled him with one shot. Near him another shouted 'Kamerad' and wisely gave up.

By the end 'the Arsenal' had fired 175 rounds of ammunition and used eleven of his grenades, destroying three enemy machine guns, killing nine Germans, shooting five others as they attempted to flee and capturing two. It was not surprising that S/Sgt Russell E. Dunham was later awarded America's highest honour, the Congressional Medal of Honor.

'The Arsenal' was the first Third Division man to win that decoration in the battle for Alsace, but he was not the only member of the Division to do so. That day another Third Division veteran was still in hospital, fighting off the gangrene which had attacked his wounded leg. For nearly a month the medics had been whittling away dead and poisoned flesh, pumping the new Second Lieutenant – he had been granted a battlefield commission just hours before he had been wounded for the second time – full of the new wonder drug penicillin.

The young officer, still limping badly, decided to visit one of his wounded sergeants in a nearby ward. Sergeant Kerrigan had been with him right from the start in Sicily, through Anzio, up to Rome, the landings in Southern France, wise-cracking, womanizing and drinking prodigious quantities of wine the whole way. Now he, too, had almost 'bought the farm' in the Vosges. But his spirits were as high as ever.

Kerrigan's back was towards the wounded lieutenant as the latter entered the ward. For a moment the young officer watched as the sergeant shuffled cards awkwardly with his bandaged hand. Then he asked innocently, 'Is this the venereal ward?'

'No, sir,' a white-faced youngster with an arm missing answered. 'This is casualty. Convalescent.'

'Then what is that syphilitic sergeant doing here?' the officer asked.

The ward fell silent. Kerrigan turned slowly. Suddenly his face lit up when he saw who was standing there. 'Why, you mule-headed, rattle-brained, scrambled-eyed whore of a lieutenant!' he exploded with delight.

Mouths dropped open. Even veteran sergeants didn't talk to officers like that. Kerrigan worked himself up to greater heights of invective, enjoying the show he was putting on for the other wounded men. 'You crawling creeping crap from Texas! You battle-happy sonofabitch!' he yelled.

'Murph,' as the officer was nicknamed, seemed to take it all in good part. Apologetically he explained to the other men, 'He never did show proper respect for officers!'

'*Respect!*' Kerrigan spat out, his face red with the effort of so much cursing, 'Why, you beagle-eared bastard, what are you doing in the rear area?'

'You'll be tickled to know that I got shot. Lost a hunk of my hip.'

Kerrigan beamed. 'Oh, Lord, to think I missed *that*!' Suddenly he rose from his bed and shot out his good hand, face wreathed in a big smile. 'Brother, am I glad to see you! You haven't changed a bit.'

Now it was 'Murph's' time to smile. 'And you're uglier than ever,' he said happily.⁹

The ward relaxed as the two began talking about old times and the combat they had seen ever since they had first met in North Africa in 1943. There the skinny son of Texan share-croppers had had to fight hard to get into the infantry and the fighting war. Now he was a veteran.

Soon their ways would part. Kerrigan would never see combat again but the young officer would. The bitter battles for Alsace would see him paying the butcher's bill in his own blood yet once more, gaining the Medal of Honor in the process of becoming the United States' most decorated soldier. Lieutenant Audie Murphy, the future Hollywood movie star, was going into battle again.¹⁰

It had been a hard week for the Supreme Commander. He had had a showdown with de Gaulle and Montgomery and had apparently lost both Bradley's and Patton's confidence on account of the Britisher's handling of the Battle of the Bulge. Although the 'Bulge' was being steadily reduced, the cost in manpower and material was very high and it was taking up a devil of a lot of time. Alsace had become a major problem as well; the Germans down there seemed able to attack where and when they liked.

Now, it appeared, another crisis was looming on the horizon because of the French First Army's inability to stop the new German drive out of the Colmar Pocket towards Strasbourg.

Eisenhower's nerves were stretched to breaking point. His health had suffered considerably and he was suffering from an old knee injury which dated back to his days at West Point. He was grasping at straws, anything which would take the pressure off his armies strung out over the 500-mile-long front.

Back in December he had dispatched his deputy, Air Chief Marshal Tedder, to Moscow on what was really a political mission. Tedder was to see Stalin and discover what the Red Army's plans were. In essence, Eisenhower wanted Stalin to go over to the offensive in the East and take the pressure off Bradley's Army Group in the Ardennes. The Tedder mission had been delayed by bad weather and on 6 January Churchill 'offered', as Eisenhower's son later phrased it in his *Bitter Woods*, to find out what Stalin was prepared to do through direct communication with the Soviet dictator. Accordingly Churchill cabled to Stalin: 'The battle in the west is very heavy and at any time large decisions may be called for from the Supreme Command. You know yourself from your own experience how very anxious the position is when a very broad front has to be defended after the temporary loss of the initiative. It is Eisenhower's great desire and need to know in outline what you plan to do, as this obviously affects all his and our major decisions. . . . I shall be grateful if you can tell me whether we can count on a major Russian offensive on the Vistula front or elsewhere during January with any other points you may care to mention. I shall not pass this most secret information to anyone except Field-Marshal Brooke and General Eisenhower and only under the condition of the utmost secrecy. I regard the matter as urgent.'[11]

By this time Stalin had already made his decision to attack. The situation was ideal for a Russian offensive, in spite of the terrible weather in the East; for most of Germany's elite formations, in particular the Panzer divisions, had been moved westwards.

But, never one to lose a political advantage or fail to ensure that a second party was indebted to him, he wrote back to Churchill a day later: 'We are preparing an offensive, but the weather is at present unfavourable. Nevertheless, taking into account the position of our Allies on the Western Front, GHQ of the Supreme Command has decided to accelerate the completion of our preparation, and, regardless of the weather, to commence large-scale offensive operations against the Germans along the whole Central Front, not later than the second half of January. You may rest assured that we shall do everything possible to render assistance to the glorious forces of our Allies.'¹²

In the German camp Colonel-General Guderian had already calculated that the great Russian offensive would start on 12 January, 1945, but Churchill thought it 'was a fine deed of the Russians and their chief to hasten their vast offensive, no doubt at a heavy cost of life',¹³ and in due course, he wrote to the cunning old dictator, who was seeking every advantage he could find for the great conference at Yalta due to take place in February, thanking him for his 'thrilling' message. He informed Stalin that he had sent a copy of his, Stalin's, letter for Eisenhower's eyes only. 'The news,' Churchill wrote, 'will be a great encouragement to General Eisenhower because it gives him the assurance that the German reinforcements will have to be split between both our flaming fronts.'¹⁴

Although Eisenhower makes no mention of this appeal to Stalin in his own book *Crusade in Europe*, the knowledge that the Russians would now be taking the pressure off them was of great moral support to the men fighting for their lives in snow-bound Alsace. As the history of the 45th Division's 179th Regiment puts it, the men 'began figuring on home in '45 again, asking (once they had learned of the Russian offensive) at breakfast, dinner and supper, "How's the Reds doing?" Spirits soared. Combat troops cracked on patrols, "Be careful if you see a bunch of guys swarming all over the hills out front – *it's probably the Russians!*" '¹⁵

It was no different in the 3rd Division. 'While the new Russian offensive in Poland may seem to be a long way from our front-line infantry platoon positions,' its G-2 Report would soon sum up, trying to reassure the men fighting in Alsace, 'it is bound to have an immediate and profound effect on the enemy capabilities in the Alsace pocket.'¹⁶

The new hope offered by the Russian offensive went so far that, when Colonel Walter Fetterly of the 44th Infantry Division was accosted by a huge Red Army officer, speaking 'in his best Mischa Auer accent' (as the 44th's *Divisional History* records), he was delighted. The 'Russian' swept his big paw across the Colonel's map of Europe and boomed, 'We have just taken all this. Now we must have a little rest.'[17] Naturally the good Colonel had been hoaxed. Not even the Red Army could advance that far that quickly. In fact the astonished officer was facing Sergeant Leonard Fooshkill of his own Operations Section, suitably disguised and dressed up as he conceived a Red Army officer might dress, complete with red sash.

When the hoax was revealed to him, Colonel Fetterly was so amused that he sent Sergeant Fooshkill up to regimental headquarters, telling his superior, Colonel Martin, that a Russian liaison officer was on his way. There the prankster promptly demanded that all minefields on the regimental front be removed so that the advancing Red Army could make contact with the Americans. 'Vun, two, three, fife days, we be in Berlin-sky,' he was recorded as having told the bemused regimental colonel, while those who were party to the hoax roared with laughter.[18]

If the hard-pressed GIs in Alsace had good reason to be thankful for Eisenhower's appeal to the Russians to begin their offensive early, the rest of Europe would, in due course, be less grateful. At Yalta, where the fate of most of Central Europe was decided, Stalin would use his supposed assistance to the Americans to build up a credit balance for himself vis-à-vis Roosevelt and Churchill. A month earlier, he argued, he had helped the Americans, at considerable cost to the Red Army. Now surely, the Americans could understand and support him. So, while the Americans slogged it out in the Ardennes and Alsace, the Red Army, facing a weakened German front in the East, hastened their drive for Vienna, Prague and Berlin and the fate of Central Europe would be determined for the rest of the century.

In the second week of January Eisenhower, now dealing for the first time *directly* with the Russian head of state, sent Stalin an eloquent telegram of congratulation on the opening of his great offensive. In Washington, General Marshall saw a copy. The Chief-of-Staff, who had done so much to promote Eisenhower's career in these last four years, told the latter coldly, 'In future, I suggest that you approach them (the Russians) in a simple Main Street, Abilene style. They are rather cynically disposed toward the diplomatic phrasing of our compliments and seem almost to appreciate downright rough talk of which I give full measure.'[19]

But the time for 'downright rough talk' to the Russian ally had not yet come. For the moment on this grey Sunday, the Supreme

Commander was concerned almost totally with the situation in the Ardennes and Alsace. That day he noted in a review that he sent to Devers and his other army commanders, that the Germans were 'fighting with great stubbornness', even the newly raised Volksgrenadier divisions, 'composed of boys and old men', who were 'only vaguely acquainted with their tasks'. There were many instances, he wrote, of men who, 'although wounded for two days, refuse to give up the fight.' There was a new fanaticism about the enemy and Eisenhower had 'no doubt that the Germans are making a supreme and all-out effort.'[20] They were and none knew it better than the GIs, as they waited in their foxholes for new battles to come.

FOUR

Dawn, Monday, 8 January, 1945.

It was cold and grey. An ominous calm lay over the Gambsheim bridgehead as the three American divisions, the 12th and 14th Armored, plus the men of the 79th Infantry Division, prepared to go over to the attack for the second time.

The 12th, the aptly named Task Force Rammer (after its commander), composed of the 56th Armored Infantry and the 714th Tank Battalion, would kick off the attack. At eleven o'clock that morning it started to assemble near the village of Rohrwiller. Almost immediately the Germans spotted the infantry and began to bring down well-aimed mortar fire on their positions. Confusion and casualties were the result. Finally, at two-thirty, the Task Force began its attack.

Meanwhile the infantry of the 79th Division were to attack south-east from Rohrwiller, with one regiment pushing towards the village of Hatten, supposedly still held in part by friendly troops. The men would be supported by an armoured battalion completely new to combat, the 827th Tank Battalion. But that wasn't all. *The tankers were black!*

In the same area of Hatten and the village of Rittershoffen, the 14th Armored would also attack, across countryside as 'smooth and as flat as a billiard table', as the 14th's *Divisional History* described it: ideal killing country for tanks on the attack.

This huge force moved forward against elements of four German divisions, the 21st Panzer, 25th Panzer Grenadier, the 47th Volksgrenadier and the 7th Parachute Division. The men at the sharp end had no illusions about what was going to happen. The Germans were in ideal offensive positions on the flat Rhine plain, criss-crossed by canals and waterways, which made it tremendously difficult country for tanks. The infantry advanced in long lines, rifles at the high port, trudging miserably through the snow and mud. The tankers squatted in the turrets of their Shermans, their eyes glued to their telescopic sights, feet tensed over the firing trigger. They knew they would get only one chance against the lurking bazooka-men or German 57mm anti-tank gun. Look away from the front for one instant and that might well be it.

So they advanced on the timbered farm houses of the target villages, the heavy brooding atmosphere broken only by the sudden angry snarl of the 500hp tank engines as a driver shifted gear for a particularly bad stretch.

At first the green 'Hellcats' of the 12th Armored's Task Force Rammer were lucky. Germans blundered right into the advancing infantry and were mown down mercilessly. A German tank scuttled across their front. It, too, was knocked out easily. Then things began to go wrong. The Task Force hit the first of the many waterways which criss-crossed the area. Enemy mortar fire started to descend upon them. Desperately they sought a bridge across. There was none. Tanks were ordered up to support an alternative plan. They would be used as mobile artillery for an assault crossing of the water. But the inexperienced 'Hellcats' had not made provision for this kind of an attack. Soon the tankers began to run out of shells. By the time dusk fell, the tanks had fired 170 HE shells and an amazing 6500 thirty-calibre machine-gun bullets! Later it was recorded that not one German casualty was found on the other side of the narrow waterway!

Thus by four-thirty the steam had run out of the attack and as the darkness increased, the tanks scuttled back to the rear for safety and the infantry were left to figure out how to cross the water on their own. In effect, the Hellcats' attack had fizzled out for that day.

At first the 79th had more luck, although one of its regiments was counterattacked by two battalions of infantry supported by tanks of the 21st Panzer Division and its main battle line was penetrated. However, the force attacking Hatten succeeded in getting into the outskirts of the village, only to find that there were Germans everywhere and the only Americans there were centred on a battalion CP, 'with one company fighting like hell to protect it', as Lieutenant Morris W. Goodwin, one of the attackers, recorded later.

Now the infantrymen requested armour to come up and give them support, even if they were black. It appeared in the form of four tank destroyers commanded by a young 2nd Lieutenant, Robert F. Jones, apparently eager to swap punches with the sixty-ton German Tiger tanks lurking in the thick smoke at the far end of the blazing, embattled village.

We can only guess what the infantrymen's first reaction to these black tankers was. In a totally segregated US Army, black soldiers were regarded by the average frontline white soldier as 'canteen commandos', 'feather merchants', who kept the supplies rolling and nothing else. In Italy a whole black division had failed in its first combat action. As late as November, 1944, Eisenhower himself thought that Negroes *couldn't* and *wouldn't* fight. It was only after realizing that he simply couldn't find enough white replacements to make up for the December losses in the Ardennes that the Supreme Commander asked for volunteers from Negro outfits to serve at the front as riflemen. Now for the first time black companies were being prepared to go into action in white regiments. So we can assume that the hard-pressed men of the 'Cross of Lorraine' Division viewed this handful of inexperienced 'coloreds' with some scepticism as they prepared to go into their first action against the Germans.

They were in for a surprise. Jones went up front personally to spot for his gunners to the rear. Taking his position on some house-steps, he spotted by firing white tracer ammunition from a machine-gun at the German tanks. A Tiger loosed a tremendous blast at the lone black. The shell tore the steps from beneath Jones. But he picked himself up and continued firing to signal the targets for his tank destroyers.

Another Tiger lumbered forward. A tank destroyer commanded by Sergeant Harry Johnson rattled up to take up the challenge. The two giants met face to face. For an instant both hesitated. But Sergeant Harry Johnson was quicker off the mark. He pressed his trigger. The tank destroyer shuddered violently. The white blur of an armour-piercing shell hurtled towards the stationary Tiger. The German commander's nerve broke. He rasped out a quick order. The sixty-ton monster's driver thrust the gear into reverse and the Tiger scuttled for cover. The situation had been saved – for the time being.

Afterwards Lieutenant Goodwin, commanding the 79th's assault company in the village, commented: 'Several of those colored boys were really wonderful, standing right there, swapping punch for punch with Tiger tanks. Their platoon leader Second Lieutenant Robert Jones deserves the Silver Star!'[1]

It is not known whether Jones ever did receive a medal. But it would probably not have made much difference in the racist America of 1945, if we are to judge from the experiences of decorated black veterans returning home that summer. Black Lieutenant Starkey, who had won the Silver Star and a battlefield commission with the black 614th Tank Battalion in Alsace, decided on his return to visit the defence plant where his wife worked and surprise her. 'I had on all my paraphernalia – battle stars, campaign ribbons, the works!' he recalled years later.

Being early, he decided to eat a hamburger at the White Tower restaurant just round the corner from the plant. But here the white counter-girl told him bluntly, 'We don't serve niggers in here!'

Starkey didn't protest, but he thought at the time: 'This is where I thought the battle should have begun, not in Alsace. Here I was supposed to be a hero returned from the war and the first thing I hear from some poor white hash-slinging trash bitch I've been fighting for: *"We don't serve niggers in here".*'[2]

As night fell over an embattled Hatten, where the Americans, whatever their colour, were now fighting for survival, a tank battalion of the enemy 25th Panzer Grenadier Division attempted a double envelopment of the village. Fifteen tanks, followed by a company of infantry, swung to the north and a similar force swung to the south. The 14th Armored's 48th Tank Battalion was immediately ordered to halt the German attack on the southern flank. They took up their positions and waited. 'We didn't have to wait long,' Lieutenant Edgar Woodward of the 48th reported later. 'Six German tanks began moving along the railroad track from Hatten. They were on our left and they apparently didn't see us, so we let them get within 600 yards and then we let go!'[3]

The first German tank was struck simultaneously by four shells. It reeled to a stop and burst into flames. Now all the Shermans opened fire. Within five minutes all the enemy tanks were knocked out and, as Woodward commented, 'they were so damned surprised they didn't fire a shot back at us'.[4]

At four that afternoon the 48th Tank Battalion and the 242nd Infantry Regiment launched yet another attack on Hatten. Corporal Franklin McGrane of the 48th remembers, 'We left our commanding ground and eased down past the Jerry tanks burning like steel torches to guide our way in the darkness. Doughfeet walked behind us, five to a tank. Now and then Heinie ammo in the flaming tanks would explode and throw hot metal into the night to make the sky a blanket of twisted colors. The night was cold; the wind was sharp. We stamped our feet on the floor of the tank. . . . From out of Hatten came a vehicle. We wet our chilled lips. One tank fired, two and three and the Jerry vehicle burst into flames. Strange and ghostlike was the scene as the flare lit up the country in the background. The gravestones glittered at us through the fire.'[5]

The Germans were not asleep in spite of that 'strange and ghostlike' scene. Almost at once the first German jets the attackers had seen came zooming out of the night sky, cannon pounding. White tracer shells streaked towards the tanks. Anti-tank guns, dug in between the half-timbered houses, thumped. Solid armour-piercing shells zipped through the glowing darkness. They were followed by the banshee howl of the dreaded 'screaming meanies', flashing high into the sky, dragging their blood-red tails after them. The enemy counterattacked and suddenly the Americans were no longer the attackers. They went to ground everywhere, as the enemy infantry and white-painted tanks rumbled towards their positions.

Corporal Todd of the 48th remembered later, 'That night the Heinies threw in a heavy barrage so that they could move tanks and infantry up under it. The fires of the burning buildings in Hatten went out and the German artillery walked up and down the field. When it got light enough to see in the morning, there were Kraut tanks painted white to blend with the snow, right in front of us! Our OD* tanks stood out like sore thumbs. I saw a Kraut tank fire at our No 5 tank and he was 75 yards away the first time I saw him! I fired once point blank at him. He went up in flames. I traversed left as quick as I could and fired two fast rounds into a second German tank. Then their artillery opened up and we were in the middle of a counter-attack again.'[6]

German tracer criss-crossed the field. A tank burst into flames. In C Company, only two tanks of its 1st Platoon escaped. The 2nd Platoon had only one left, the 3rd Platoon three. In the end C Company, or what was left of it, was ordered to withdraw. Now B Company came rumbling up to take its share of the punishment. They crossed the field under artillery fire successfully, but the German anti-tank guns on the other side were waiting for the Shermans. Sergeant Winslow, platoon sergeant of B's Third Platoon recalled, 'As my section crossed we were

---

* Olive drab.

fired on from somewhere to the south of Hatten. Behind me Captain Elder's tank was hit twice in quick succession. Four more tanks were hit and still we couldn't pick up the flashes. It's a strange feeling to see a shower of sparks cover the turret of the tank in front of you. Your whole body goes tense, you're scared to your fingertips.'[7]

But it was no good. B Company couldn't make it either. With five tanks already hit, it was ordered to withdraw as well. The 48th Tank Battalion's attack had come to an end for that day.

In Hatten itself, the infantry of the 242nd Regiment of the Rainbow Division and the survivors of the 79th Infantry Division still slogged it out bitterly with the attacking Germans. Master sergeants are not normally found in the front line, but this day in Hatten, there was no front line. Thus it was that Master Sergeant Vito Bertoldo of the 242nd found himself guarding a CP in the open street for twelve hours against determined German attacks by both infantry and armour. At 75 yards range the German Tigers blasted away at the lone American firing his machine-gun from a kitchen table with their mighty 88mm cannon. Once two German half-tracks unloaded infantry, as a tank rumbled towards the CP. Calmly Bertoldo waited for the grenadiers to get out, then he let them have a burst. They went flying like ninepins. Twenty of them were mown down. A colonel gave the order for the CP to be withdrawn. Bertoldo volunteered to stay behind to cover the withdrawal. He stayed there alone all night. He had been on his feet fighting for nearly twenty-four hours. Still he did not weaken. He moved his machine gun inside a building being used as the CP of another trapped battalion. There he defended the position all day long. Once he broke up a whole infantry attack, led by a German 88mm self-propelled gun. But during this attack he was seriously wounded. Still he remained at his post. It was decided to evacuate this second CP post. The Germans were pressing in from all sides. Again Bertoldo volunteered to cover the withdrawal. At the same instant that the Americans began to pull back, the Germans attacked. They poured a withering barrage into the buildings all around. Undaunted, Bertoldo remained at his post, hurling white phosphorous grenades at the advancing infantry until they finally broke and fled. A German tank rattled up. At less than fifty yards from where the lone soldier was still holding out, it let fly. The shell blew Bertoldo right across the room and destroyed his machine gun. Even now he continued the unequal fight, holding off the advancing Germans with his remaining weapon – *a rifle!* In the end, after forty-eight hours of combat, in which he had killed forty German soldiers and wounded many more, Sergeant Bertoldo allowed himself to be evacuated. He was awarded the Medal of Honor for tremendous courage against overwhelming odds.

That day what was left of the first American battalion to be overrun at Hatten was ordered to withdraw to the positions of the 79th's 315th Regiment. Only a couple of hundred of them could be mustered to proceed to the rear; weary, unshaven, they started to pass through the lines of the 315th, glad to be out of it for the time being. But not all of them – twenty volunteered to stay behind and fight on with the 315th. Flatly they told the 315th's officers, 'We've run far enough. We're not going to run any further!'[8]

Not far away in Herrlisheim the 12th Armored Division were also fighting for survival. There the 56th Armored Infantry Battalion had been cut off, its communications with the rear severed. German prisoners reported that the *Amis* in Herrlisheim had been wiped out. Thirty-odd Americans from the same battalion, either deserters or genuine stragglers, also reached the rear, claiming that their battalion had been cut off and wiped out.

The 'Hellcat' officers didn't give up hope. A counterattack was ordered in an attempt to reach Herrlisheim. Somehow the Shermans managed to break through to find that there were troops still fighting, although the battalion commander and most of his officers were wounded. Every one of the houses held by the Americans was packed with casualties. The tankers realized that they would have to withdraw. Artillery was called up. The 105mms started shelling the outskirts of the village dead on time. Meanwhile the tanks were hurriedly loaded with their groaning bundles of misery. Orders were given that the tankers were not to start up their motors until the very last moment. The wounded would go out first. The surviving infantry would cover their withdrawal. To their rear the guns continued to thunder. To their front the sky was as bright as day. Finally the tanks were ready. The Shermans began to move out.

Freezing fog began to descend upon the escapers, but for once they were glad of it. It provided the cover they needed. The infantry at the rear grabbed hold of each other's belts and staggered on, totally exhausted, like blind men. Would the Germans spot them? That was the thought uppermost in all their minds. But luck was on their side that night. Only one tank to their front was hit. Otherwise the Germans did not seem aware that they were escaping from the trap.

One hour after they had started they crossed the River Zorn, from which they had begun their attack so hopefully two days before, and began wearily to dig in. The 12th Armored Division's first attempt to capture Herrlisheim had failed miserably.

The men were tiring rapidly. The freezing weather seemed endless. At times the GIs in the line were more concerned with simple survival in the coldest winter in a quarter of a century than with the enemy. The infantry lived like animals, burying into small holes in the frozen earth in a vain attempt to find warmth. They let their beards grow. They were filthy dirty, and often hungry too. The loss of their shoepaks meant they got frostbite or trench foot; and there were cases recorded of men doing exactly that – exposing their feet to the icy wind in order to be evacuated.

Water was a problem although the men were surrounded by deep snow. Canteens froze to solid chunks of ice. K-ration cans had to be tucked under shirts and armpits to prevent their contents freezing up. A warm meal was a rarity and even when the cooks did manage to bring up cooked food, it was usually cold by the time it reached the foxholes.

In the 70th Division that second week of January, the future minister, Donald Docken, wrote to his parents: 'Things have been pretty hot for us in the past two weeks and I haven't been able to get a letter off. My mind is absolutely stripped of any traces of reason for war – as if there was any in the first place. Maybe the overall picture justifies what goes on up here, but, from an infantryman's point of view, it is hard to see. A lot of friends are not here any more, which is a terrible reminder of the evil of war. It makes more solemn the fact they should not die in vain. Every once in a while I have to stop and justify what goes on here by thinking of the great cause we are fighting for.'[9]

Some simply could not take it. They avoided combat by going sick or pleading nerves. Or they just ran away. As Private Jones of the 70th Division recorded after the battle: 'There were those of us who went where we had to and tried to get the job done; others loved the adventure of war and the killing; others were cowards. It was these last, officers and men alike, who made life rough on the rest of us. . . . I had a great respect for Colonel Barten (his CO) and sympathy – if privates can have sympathy for battalion commanders – for the terrible task he had in trying to get his battalion to fight effectively.'[10]

The problem of making the Seventh Army units in the line an effective fighting force was known at higher headquarters. In the second week of January the combat efficiency reports of the six divisions regularly under General Brooks' command were not particularly encouraging. Only two of his divisions, neither of which had yet seen combat in the current battle, the 103rd and the veteran 36th, were rated as 'very satisfactory'. Three were described as merely 'satisfactory' and one, the 12th Armored Division, was rated 'unsatisfactory'.[11]

Every one of the formations actually engaged in battle was reported to be suffering from combat fatigue and seriously under-strength, which was only too true. By the end of January, eleven of Brooks' divisions, and those of Wade Haislip's Corps, had lost between ten and twenty percent of their effectives, in the rifle companies losses rising to forty and fifty percent. In all a total of 15,275 men were reported killed, wounded, missing and captured.

Soon General Patch, commander of the Seventh Army, had to tell General Devers that he didn't think that Brooks' Sixth Corps could hold the enemy if he attacked again.

PART III

Withdrawal

'The children, always a barometer of native feeling, began to hurl icy snowballs at the troops. The soldiers didn't care much. "We deserve it," they thought.'

History of the US 103rd Division

ONE

'King Jean' was puzzled. Throughout the previous day the German Nineteenth Army had been attacking relentlessly out of the Colmar Pocket, trying to extend their salient, creeping ever nearer to Strasbourg. On Wednesday his exhausted battalions fought, in some cases to the last man, in an attempt to prevent the Germans crossing the River Ill. Against the vital village of Obenheim, General Wiese, 'King Jean's' opponent since the August landings in Southern France, had attacked with five battalions of infantry and numerous tanks. All day the battle had swayed back and forth. Once the Germans had sent in envoys under a flag of truce offering the Frenchmen an honourable surrender. They had refused, in spite of tremendous casualties and the fact that they were rapidly running out of supplies. At midday twin-engined Marauder bombers had been sent in. In spite of the terrible weather and the German flak they had zoomed in low to drop seventy-two containers of food and ammunition to the trapped defenders. Unfortunately most of the parachutes had been carried by the strong wind into the German positions.

All afternoon 'King Jean' had followed over the radio the desperate attempts of the garrison to hold the village. By eight in the evening the tanks of the *Feldherrnhalle* Brigade were in Obenheim itself. One hour later they were in control of the central crossroads. Two hours later the radio fell silent and 'King Jean' knew that Colonel Coffinier's battalion holding Obenheim existed no more. In the end only two officers and a score of men out of nearly 600 managed to sneak out of the doomed village under the cover of darkness. That had been on Wednesday, 10 January. But on Thursday, with German prisoners reporting that across the Rhine Himmler was preparing to send two new SS divisions to General Wiese's aid, nothing happened in the new salient.

Early that morning de Lattre had told his Corps Commander, General de Monsabert, that 'it is necessary at all costs to maintain the integrity of the Ill position from Krafft to Ebersheim during the coming days'.[1] He also ordered all available reserves in the rear to be alerted to move to bar the Vosges passes at a moment's notice, in case the Germans tried to a new tack. 'All were awaiting the new rush,' wrote de Lattre after the war, 'which did not turn up.'[2] Puzzled and not a little worried, 'King Jean', accompanied as always by a cluster of elegant aides and flunkies, motored to General Devers' HQ at Vittel. There the Commander of the French First Army expressed his doubts to Devers: Why this sudden halt? Was it because of the extent of their losses? Or the tiredness of the German units? Or perhaps the absence of reserves, or the fear that there might be need of them in the south of the Colmar Pocket? Or dissension in command – argument between the military and Himmler on how the battle should be conducted?[3]

The two Generals tossed the theories back and forth without coming to any firm conclusion. In the end, de Lattre let it go, concluding, as he wrote later, 'that the main thing is that the magnificent resistance in barring the route south of Strasbourg to the Germans had contributed to protecting the cathedral spire from the new defilement of the red flag and the swastika'.[4] In fact, that which General Brooks had been fearing ever since he had received the reports on the state of his command had happened: his tired Sixth Corps had been attacked again.

On the Wednesday, as the battle raged below Strasbourg, General Petersen, commanding the German XV Corps, readied his corps for the new surprise attack in the north. His corps consisted of the three Volksgrenadier divisions, the 361st, 36th, the 256th, and the 10,000 men of the Sixth Mountain Division, which had now finally arrived at the front. These four divisions, with the SS in the lead, would strike General Frederick's 45th Infantry Division, break through it, and attempt once again to gain the vital passes through the Vosges. This time the Germans were determined to make a link-up with their various salients to the south-east and south in order to cut off the Seventh Army and finally seal the fate of Northern Alsace and, with luck, Strasbourg too.

At seven o'clock on the morning of 11 January the first wave of SS men came rushing out of the woods behind a massive rolling barrage of artillery and mortar fire. The veterans of the 45th opened fire at once. The men of the Sixth's Second Battalion, some six hundred strong, fell writhing in the snow. But there was no stopping these young men, mostly in their teens and early twenties, who had been steeped in the Nazi creed since they had been in short pants. As the morning passed in murder and mayhem, they forced the 'Thunderbirds' back yard by yard. In the end the veterans yielded six hundred yards to the SS.

A counterattack was ordered. Badly mauled and battered as they were, the Americans counterattacked and gained back the ground they had lost. But that was all. The SS started to dig in and a battle began between the SS and the Thunderbirds which, as the *Divisional History* testifies, 'was one of the severest tests faced in its history'.[5] For the men the Thunderbirds were now fighting regarded themselves as the Third Reich's elite. These young soldiers of the SS bore on their belt buckles, not the traditional *Wehrmacht* legend '*Gott mit uns*' (God with us), but the new oath '*Unsere Ehre heisst Treue*' (our honour is loyalty). That loyalty was to the Führer and was rarely broken. Rarely did the American troops capture an SS officer alive and even the rank-and-file surrendered mostly only when they were wounded. Most of them deemed it an honour to die in battle.

The battle swayed back and forth over the snow-bound fields and hills littered with the dead of both sides. Marching into yet another desperate counterattack, Master Sergeant Maurice Cohen of the 45th's hard-pressed 157 Infantry Regiment thought, 'It was the worst mess I ever saw. Dead and wounded Americans and Germans were lying all over the area. We had no way of evacuating the wounded, much less the dead.'[6]

Pfc William Sain, wounded in the same action, recalled after the war, 'Those damned Heinies counterattacked in rushes. Enemy dead were piled up like cordwood in front of our positions.'[7] But still the young fanatics of the SS kept attacking, and not always frontally. Using the tactics they had learned in those remote Finnish woods, they started to infiltrate behind the 157's Third Battalion. Like timber wolves, they sneaked through the firs, slipping in in small groups, digging in so that soon they were established *behind* the Third in company strength.

For a while the CO of the Third didn't know that he was virtually cut off to the rear. Then a ration train of three jeeps heading for the Third was ambushed. One of the four survivors, Corporal Alfred Miller, later gasped out what had happened: 'I'd just returned from the hospital and was riding up with the ration train to rejoin the company. We rounded a bend in the road and suddenly came under direct machine-gun and rifle fire. We all hit the ditch on the other side of the road and I rolled down an embankment until I reached a covered position. After covering the road with small arms and machine-gun fire which riddled the ration trucks, the Germans began firing rifle grenades at the men on the ground. I saw one man take a direct hit in the face and fall over dead. Grenades fell near my position and I crawled to another without being hit. By crawling and running from one place to another, I got back to our lines.'[8]

Now began the ordeal of the trapped Third Battalion, cut off from the rear in dense forest country, just as Major Whittesley's famed 'Lost Battalion' had been, not too far away in the Argonne Forest twenty-seven years before. The Third Battalion would hold out, too, for well over a week. But it would *not* be relieved in the nick of time as had the 'Lost Battalion'. It would go down fighting, beaten in the end by those fanatical young men with their tarnished skull-and-crossbone cap badges. Only two men were to escape of the five companies of American infantrymen involved.

That same morning that the SS infiltrated the rear of the 45th's 3rd Battalion, the whole of the 14th Armored Division was thrown into the attack against the Hatten-Rittershoffen salient. There were no reserves. All three combat commands were going to be used in one last desperate attempt to stop the Germans. The history of the 14th Armored records: 'The men moved up to the line of departure, leaving the friendly Alsatian towns, laughing. For many of them it would be their last laughter.'[9] Indeed it would. By the time the defeated 14th Armored was finally withdrawn from the Hatten-Rittershoffen salient, eighty-three officers and 1038 enlisted men, nearly one tenth of the division's strength, had been killed, wounded, or missing in action. The Germans were waiting for them. They followed the armored infantrymen of the 62nd Battalion to form up in open ground prior to the attack. Then they opened up with everything they had. It wasn't war; it was a massacre. Wounded men dropped screaming to the ground and were frozen to death where they lay. Others were ripped apart by the intense shelling. Later the black soldiers of the Graves

Registration details collected the pieces in buckets, hoping to find dogtags among the gory mess. The 62nd tried to push on, but it was useless. In 'A' company seventy men had become casualties in less than an hour, two-thirds of its strength. Eyes wild with shock, the survivors straggled back in twos and threes and began to dig in. It was recorded that it took some of them six hours to dig a foxhole in which to shelter; the ground was that hard.

It was the same with every one of the 14th Armored's battalions attacking that day, and it was the massed fire of seven whole artillery battalions which saved the attackers from even worse losses.

More and more of the new German jets hissed in to shoot up the infantry and tanks below, clearly outlined against the snow. Losses started to mount rapidly. The Division threw in its last troops, the 47th Tank Battalion and the 19th Infantry. Their attack ran into trouble right from the start; they knew neither the terrain nor the number or quality of the enemy to their front. All the same the mixed force reached within 300 yards of the village of Hatten when a devastating hail of small arms and artillery fire struck the attackers. Tank after tank was hit. Casualties mounted rapidly. As Pfc James Benniger remembered afterwards, 'It was hell. The sickening sight of a helmet spinning over forty feet in the air' – the result of a direct hit by an 88mm shell.[10]

It was no good. The companies were ordered to withdraw. As they started pulling back everyone was carrying or helping to carry a wounded comrade. The situation became ever more critical. More and more pockets of the broken battalion were trapped and either surrendered or fought to the end. But in the midst of the mayhem there was a kind of grim humour. As the wounded piled up in a dugout, a Captain Spokes cracked, 'I'll have to sign a statement of charges for the carbine I lost, I guess,' and he held up the gory stump of the hand which had been holding the lost weapon.[11]

Now Hatten was ablaze, casting ugly crimson shadows over the snowy fields. Inside the village, in the confused, chaotic fighting all hell was let loose. Systematically the Germans set fire to the remaining buildings with incendiary bullets. One crazed German turned the nozzle of his flame-thrower into a cellar packed with women and children. Their frantic screams could be heard even above the thunder of the guns and the racket kicked up by the tank engines.

'Why don't you Yankee bastards give up!' the infuriated Germans

yelled as they attacked house after house. A German opened the door
of one of the houses occupied by the American survivors. '*Kamerad!*'
he yelled and flung up his hands. 'Come in,' the Americans cried
at the same moment that the German stepped to one side to let the
other German behind him spray the room with his burp gun. The
attackers didn't get far. Men fell everywhere. Under covering fire
from C Company they withdrew, leaving the street littered with their
dead.

Captain Young, CO of C Company, was called to battalion HQ.
There a staff officer, Major Green, told him, 'Young, you'll have to
make the attack since E Company has failed.'

'Sir, how do you think my men will feel after seeing what happened
to Easy Company?' Major Green could see he might have trouble on
his hands.

'All right, we'll see Colonel Holton.' Together they went down the
steps into the smoky cellar, lit by a couple of candles, which was
the CO's command post. Holton listened to what Green had to say
and then he rounded on Young. 'Charley Company WILL attack,' he
bellowed, red in the face.

Miserably, Young went back to his Company to tell them the bad
news. 'Are we the only goddam company in the Army?' one platoon
leader complained. Young cut the moaning short. 'We're going
anyway.'[12]

Surprisingly enough C Company made its attack without a single
casualty, but their luck didn't last long. Half an hour later the Germans
counterattacked and C Company started to lose men rapidly. Again
the miserable procession of bloody, broken men started wending its
way to the rear, followed by enemy mortar fire. A half-track, clearly
marked with the red cross, and piled high with wounded was hit. An
aidman helping to carry back a litter cried suddenly, 'Look out, I'm
going to drop it!' Someone snarled, 'Why don't you use two hands?'
'I can't,' the litter man answered and held up his right arm. The hand
had just been shot off.

It was no better on the sector of the bridgehead held by the 12th
Armored Division. For the second time the 'Hellcats' entered the ruins
of Herrlisheim and for the second time they suffered disaster there.
The 17th Armored Infantry Battalion was surrounded in the shattered
village and had to withdraw hurriedly, losing officers and men who
had no other recourse but surrender. At Herrlisheim, too, a major
portion of the 43rd Tank Battalion became 'missing in action'. The

43rd, which had already lost twelve tanks in the action at Offendorf the previous day, followed the decimated 17th Armored Infantry into Herrlisheim. At noon its Commanding Officer radioed, 'Things are pretty hot here'. That was the last that was heard of him and most of his battalion. After the war it was reported that fourteen of his tanks were knocked out and fifteen were listed, strangely enough, as 'missing'. The *Divisional History* records laconically only that the '43rd was reorganized under a new commanding officer'.[13] In fact the greenhorns of the 12th Armored Division had run into an elite formation with disastrous consequences, the 10th SS Panzer Division *'Hohenstauffen'*, the victors of Arnhem.

The 10th SS had fought brilliantly in Russia, had been shattered in Normandy, and had then taken part with the 9th SS Panzer Division in the slaughter of the British 1st Airborne Division at Arnhem in September, 1944. In fact, it can be said that the 10th SS Panzer had gained Germany's only real victory on the Western Front in 1944. Now, after resting out the Battle of the Bulge in Germany, it had begun crossing the Rhine by ferry in the second week of January. Its crossing was disturbed by constant Allied dive-bombing attacks and by mines which the French floated down the river from Strasbourg. In fact the mines were worse than the dive-bombers and the SS had been forced to station machine-gunners on the banks of the river to knock them out. One ferry was blown up by such a floating bomb and the men of the SS Panzer Grenadier Regiment 22 had been forced to swim the broad river through freezing water, heavily laden with equipment. Not a few never made it.

When *Obersturmführer* Bachmann, a typical dashing, energetic SS officer, commanding the lead element, discovered that his men were being 'held up', as he phrased it later, by the *Amis* he got on his motorbike and raced up to see what was the matter. Like most SS officers, who always suffered higher losses than *Wehrmacht* officers, Bachmann liked to command from the front. Skidding to a stop on the outskirts of Herrlisheim he was confronted by a Sherman. Its cannon belched fire and Bachmann ducked for cover. But not for long. Crawling back through the snow, he grabbed the *panzerfaust* strapped to the side-car. Now he stalked the thirty-ton tank until he got within thirty metres of it. He didn't hesitate, although he knew he was armed with a one-shot weapon and if he failed to knock it out with this shot, he was a dead man. He put the cheap 'throw-away' tube on his shoulder and squinted through the sight. The Sherman seemed to fill the whole world. He could see the white star on its sides, the bundles of equipment hanging from the turret, even the rusty rivets. He pressed the trigger. The tube bounced on his shoulder. Flame shot out of its rear end and the ugly bottle-shaped bomb started to wobble its way towards the unsuspecting *Ami*. The Sherman gave a great lurch as if struck by a sudden tornado. An instant later it was blazing fiercely. Bachmann's tanks started moving forward once more. A second Sherman was knocked out. Total confusion seemed to reign in the enemy camp.

An American officer doubled forward, hands raised. He wanted to surrender. Bachmann was only too glad to oblige him. The American officer surrendered not only himself, but sixty other 'Hellcats' and twenty Germans they had taken prisoner. Bachmann now had time to question his prisoner. 'I asked him,' he reported after the war, 'whether he was the commander of the two Shermans just knocked out.

'To my surprise he answered, "No, I'm in charge of those four" and indicated four Shermans standing in a yard, which I hadn't noticed up to now.'[4]

Bachmann reacted immediately. He ordered all American drivers to step forward out of the line of prisoners. Obligingly enough several of them did just that. Swiftly he allotted each *Ami* a grinning SS guard. The Americans and Germans took possession of the four Shermans and started up their motors. Another eight Shermans were seized and driven to the rear, while the two Panthers now under Bachmann's command knocked out a further seven. As that day ended, a triumphant Bachmann could report that he had captured sixty prisoners, plus twelve Shermans and knocked out a further seven, a grand total of nineteen enemy tanks. That is what happened to the Hellcats' unfortunate 43rd Tank Battalion.

In due course the bold young SS officer, *Obersturmführer* Bachmann, was awarded the coveted Knight's Cross of the Iron Cross for his exploits by a grateful Führer and thus 'cured his throatache',* as they said in the Waffen SS.

Virtually two entire battalions of the 12th Armored Division had been decimated at Herrlisheim and the manpower barrel had been

---

* Because the Knight's Cross was worn round the neck. Once the neck was covered by the black and white ribbon of the award, one's 'throatache' was cured.

scraped almost clean. The Hellcats' days in the Battle of Alsace were numbered.

It was no better at Hatten and Rittershoffen, where the 79th Division supported by the tanks of the 14th Armored hung on desperately to the bits of those villages which they had captured at such great cost.

Captain Persky, leading a counterattack with all available tanks, trying to support the infantry, recalled after the war, how he couldn't see anything. 'The smoke was too bad.' Three of his tanks were knocked out in quick succession. Then he burst through the smoke and gasped, 'Christ, there are millions of them up here. They're everywhere.' Then he went off the air. The shell with his 'number on it' had finally found him. Fortunately Captain Persky survived, though badly wounded. Almost immediately the Germans counterattacked. As always, first came the artillery bombardment, then the quick grey shapes of enemy infantry running into the attack, then the machine-guns chattering savagely, then they were in the houses and the old, old ritual of mayhem and violent death began again.

'You could hear the shouts and the screams through the gun fire,' the *Divisional History* recorded, 'and the screams of the women trapped in the cellar of a burning house, set afire by white phosphorus. . . . "Counterattacks in the Hatten area were beaten off today" was the way the news despatches read but that did not tell of the artillery fire and what a counterattack was. That did not tell you of the death and the screaming, the sweating in that cold air and the suffering, all that cannot be put on paper.'[15]

Back at the rear the supply troops and the like sent up their Christmas packages and anything else they could scrounge to help out with the trapped GIs' rations. They shot rabbits and stole chickens from the peasants to send forward. But even they were under attack. The Germans seemed to be everywhere. As one divisional history recorded, 'There was no safe place, no safe way to do anything'.

In Hatten the wounded were piling up, for there was no way of evacuating them. The Army Air Corps tried to fly low-level missions to drop much-needed medical supplies, but the intense German flak drove them off. The artillery attempted to fire shells containing drugs and bandages into Hatten and the other beleaguered villages, but it didn't work. Somehow or other, however, individual supply sergeants managed to get through down remote snowbound trails of their own finding, brave unknown men who would never be decorated. So weary were the infantrymen that they did not even have the strength to make the traditional wisecrack as they opened up yet another of the little olive-drab cans, '*And which one* has got the cunt in it?'

By now, as the 14th Armored's history records: 'The dead lying in the street began to get on your nerves and the tenseness of always having to look down the sights (of a tank), always waiting and the artillery always coming in and it was only a question of time before one landed on the house you were in. . . . The fighting had reached such a viciousness that they tried to range in eight-inch howitzers on single houses, which is like trying to hit a fly with a shotgun.'[16]

Thousands of shells, German and American, churned up the rubble time and time again. In Hatten alone 420 men, many of them wounded, were trapped in the cellars, lying packed together with their dead. As the *Divisional History* states, 'the men were physically and mentally exhausted'.[17]

A German patrol dressed in American uniforms penetrated into the cellar occupied by Lieutenant Charles Bailey and part of his C Company in Hatten.

'Are there Americans in there?' a voice demanded in English. When Bailey answered 'yes', the Germans sprayed the cellar with machine pistol fire and tossed in concussion grenades. Lieutenant Bailey was wounded, but the rest of his company rallied quickly. The enemy patrol was wiped out mercilessly.

It was becoming clear that the Americans could hold these shattered villages not much longer. Volunteers were asked for to form defensive screens around them. Withdrawal, or worse, was in the air. The engineers were secretly ordered to lay a minefield, the biggest they would ever lay. It was to stretch right across the front of the 14th Armored Division. But mines, like shells, were in short supply. In the end the engineers received over six thousand unfamiliar British land mines. They laid them, in spite of the fact that they were constantly under enemy artillery fire, two hundred yards away from known German positions. One man stumbled carrying four of the British mines. He was killed outright and two men near him were wounded. Still the engineers laboured on, knowing that time was running out.

The bridges to the rear were prepared for demolition. Trees were hastily notched and packets of TNT put in place, ready to be blown so that the trees would form elementary road blocks. Infantry were sent forward to string out barbed-wire emplacements. The Alsatians got the message. The Americans were going back. Here and there they decided, in spite of the intense barrage, to pull out before the great withdrawal started. Thus it was that the engineers saw an Alsatian family, elderly father, mother and young daughter, who tried to get from Rittershoffen to Hatten. They had a cart, drawn by two oxen, on which were all their household goods. They received a direct hit by a mortar.[18]

Somehow the Germans seemed to sense what was going on. They became even bolder, pressing home their advantage, knowing that the *Amis* were soon going to run. Perhaps the many German sympathizers known to be in the Rhine-bank villages were still supplying them with information. In the 79th Infantry Division's area alone fifty German spies were rounded up during the battle, and virtually every regimental or divisional history records some instance of an Alsatian civilian spotting for the enemy. In Hatten the Germans were particularly active, attacking time and again with infantry armed with the most fearsome weapon of all – flame-throwers. It was no different at Rittershoffen, where, with nearly half the men of the 79th Division's 315th Infantry Regiment evacuated as casualties, the survivors held on grimly. They even impressed the attacking Germans as a Major Kurz, captured at the end of the war, records: 'I never thought much of Americans as soldiers,' he told his interrogators, 'until I fought them at Rittershoffen, but there we found them an antagonist who defended bitterly and with more determination than we had previously seen the Americans demonstrate'.[19]

But in spite of all their courage and determination, it was about over. On 19th January the 10th SS Panzer Division hit the Second Battalion of the Cross of Lorraine's 314th Regiment in full force. They attacked the Americans' positions at Drusenheim with two battalions of infantry and a large number of tanks. For three hours the men of the Cross of Lorraine held out. As darkness fell, news was received to the rear that the Second was completely surrounded. Orders were given to break out. It failed disastrously. Only one hundred men out of six hundred-odd managed to escape; the rest died or surrendered. Yet another American battalion had been wiped out.

That last disaster seemed to act as a signal for both sides. The Germans redoubled their attacks. Patch, reviewing his losses, an average of fifteen percent per unit, and remembering that he had to list the 12th Armored, Task Force Linden (42nd Infantry Division) and Task Force Herren (70th Infantry Division) as 'unsatisfactory', with the two latter formations in need of 'additional unit training', decided he couldn't hold all his front. It was obvious the enemy was massing for a new attack everywhere. Combat fatigue and losses were plaguing all his formations; could they withstand a renewed assault? Patch decided they couldn't. That day he informed General Devers in Vittel that he could not hold the front as it stood. Devers gave the order that Eisenhower had wanted him to give back at the New Year. Brooks' Sixth Corps would retire to the line of the River Moder, which flows out of the Vosges and along the southern edge of the Haguenau Forest to the Rhine. Here the Sixth would set up a new defensive line, curving to the south between Bischwiller and Weyersheim, where de Lattre's First French Army sector began.

For any red-blooded American soldier, used to gaining ground and not giving it up whatever the pressure from the enemy, the order was going to be hard to obey. But both Patch and Brooks knew there was no alternative. Sixth Corps could take no further punishment of the kind it had been taking for the last three weeks. Although Patch observed to Brooks, 'I think he (the enemy) is getting tired. I think we will be able to hang on all right'[20], both Generals knew that the Germans had plenty of fight in them yet. It was wiser to get the troops out while there was still time.

The men in the line thought the same, however angry or sad they were to give up ground they had fought so hard for. Preparing the bridge between Niederbetschdorf and Rittershoffen for demolition, prior to the great withdrawal, the men of the 68th Infantry Regiment described later the end of Rittershoffen, just after they pulled out for good: 'You heard shouting and stifled screams and the identifying brrrrp brrrp of Jerry guns, the steady cracking of machine guns and small arms fire coming from the windows, crevices, the church steeple, the deep rumble of tanks. Some tanks no longer moved, black hulks among the charred ruins of homes. White phosphorous shells burst in the streets, with sudden yellow flames and smoke pouring from half-timber buildings. Buildings that only smoked because there was nothing more to burn made the town look like a ghost town, and still the shells came in. The mortars that never gave a warning, endlessly plopping in, scattering mortar and rubbish. There was the catching voice, crying "Medic!" The surrounding fields no longer had a mantle of clear white snow. It was now stained with soot from powder, pock-marked with craters and soiled with blood.'[21])

It was the same everywhere in those ruined Alsatian villages as the exhausted Americans prepared to pull back, leaving the civilians, pro-German or anti-Nazi, it didn't matter now, to their fate. Later there would be much criticism of the Americans by the French. But it would be conveniently forgotten that Eisenhower had authorized the same withdrawal nearly three weeks earlier! Only de Gaulle's intervention and his concern about the fate of Strasbourg had stayed the Supreme Commander's hand. Now Strasbourg was virtually saved. But in the meantime some ten thousand young Americans had paid the price for the maintenance of French national pride.

TWO

The 45th Division's 'Lost Battalion' had nearly reached the end of its tether. For nearly a week the trapped men had been holding out on the hillside positions against the SS. There, some two miles north-west of the little village of Reipertswiller, some seven hundred men boxed in on Height 348 had hung on desperately, hoping, as each new dawn illuminated the lunar landscape of shell-holes and dead bodies, that relief would come that day.

Once, a brave young officer, Lieutenant Willis Talkington, had loaded a light tank with rations, ammunition and medical supplies and had fought his way through the SS lines. But trying to return the next morning, it was knocked out. All the tankers were killed and Lieutenant Talkington wounded, though he managed to struggle back to his own lines.

On the 18th the Germans attacked in force. G Company was overrun, with only thirty men escaping death or capture. Now the jubilant SS moved in their celebrated mountain artillery and started pounding the Third Battalion's unprotected flanks. Casualties began to mount rapidly. One of the two survivors of the 'Lost Battalion' reported later: 'The enemy artillery and mortar fire out there was the worst I'd ever seen. At least three-quarters of the men on the hill had a wound of some kind and a few had two or three. Until the last day we placed the wounded in holes with the other unwounded so that men who weren't hurt could guard them and give them aid. We had no medical supplies, no food, and no heat to melt the snow for water. Once we found a box of rations underneath an ammunition pile. We gave the rations only to the wounded.'[1]

The 45th's First Battalion was ordered to attack and break through to the trapped 'Thunderbirds'. They had hardly started when they were pinned down by enemy fire. A withdrawal was ordered and the SS, as always lightning-quick off the mark, rushed six machine guns into the gap left by the withdrawing Americans. The Second attacked again, but was mown down by the fire of those six machine guns. That was the end of the Second's attempt to relieve the 'Lost Battalion'.

All communication with the men on Height 348 broke down, save by radio. It was impossible to maintain land lines in that constant bombardment which both sides kept up. By 18 January the divisional artillery were firing a staggering total of 5000 high explosive shells daily in order to offer some protection to the trapped men. General Frederick, the Divisional Commander, ordered the 157th Regiment to which the 'Lost Battalion' belonged to hold its positions as long as possible in order not 'to show weakness'.

A composite group of anti-tank gunners and heavy weapons men were thrown into the attack. They succeeded in knocking out some of the SS machine guns but were soon bogged down by intense enemy fire like all those who had tried before them. One of them, S/Sgt Bernard Fleming, a squad leader, recalled after the war: 'My squad was in a ditch with three enemy machine guns on us. I asked for a volunteer to get aid. He got only about fifty yards when a machine gun killed him. I asked for another and he got about ten yards before he was shot through the legs. I went out and dragged him behind some cover, then yelled to the others that I was going to the rear myself. I don't know how I made it, but I did. I saw Colonel Sparks and told him what had happened.'[2]

Colonel Sparks, who commanded the 'Lost Battalion', but who had not been trapped with his men, was desperate. Single-handed he took over a tank and drove through the mud and snow to Fleming's trapped squad. Personally manning a 30-calibre machine gun, he fired a staggering 5000 rounds of ammunition at the enemy, while directing the tank's big 76mm cannon. Somehow he managed to get the squad to shelter and then, seeing other wounded men lying helpless in a ditch, he jumped off the tank and personally carried them back to the Sherman and safety.

Still the slaughter went on. That night the Second Battalion of the 411th Infantry Regiment was brought up. On the morrow it would attack and relieve the 'Lost Battalion'. Hurriedly they were briefed on their mission and the enemy's strength – and it wasn't pleasant hearing: 'The enemy's infiltration has enabled them to build up a line of estimated company strength in which a number of automatic weapons are emplaced and which is outposted by machine-gun positions. In many places in this line enemy forces are dug in under the rocks on the slopes of hills and because of the accuracy of the artillery and rocket fire brought down when any attempt is made to dislodge these troops, it is believed that there are artillery observers in this line, providing the support fire so necessary to its existence.'[3]

At dawn on 20 January, a day of snowfall and freezing wind, the men of the 411th's Second Battalion prepared to move out. Their chances were slim. They were fighting not only a fanatical enemy, well dug in and armed with multiple automatic weapons, supported by artillery, but the appalling weather too. They kicked off in a raging snow storm and as the *History of the 157th Regiment* records laconically, 'They were cut down!'

Hastily the battalion was reorganized, officers and NCOs shaking the shocked men into some sort of skirmish line. Once more, at noon, they set off again across the bare snowy fields, littered with their own dead, like bundles of abandoned rags, pocked here and there by smoking brown shell-holes like a work of giant moles. They didn't stand a chance. As the 157th Regiment records yet again, 'They were stopped cold.'

Now, virtually all hope of contacting the 'Lost Battalion' had vanished. Colonel O'Brien, commanding the 157th Regiment, tried frantically to obtain air support for his trapped men. But although the Air Corps were prepared to brave the German flak and have another go at trying to re-supply the 'Lost Battalion', the weather stubbornly refused to give them a break. All afternoon it continued to snow and sleet, with visibility down to two hundred yards.

Some time that afternoon O'Brien received a message from General Frederick ordering him to pull out the 157th. It was soon to be relieved of its mission in order to reorganize and fill out the gaps in its ranks after three weeks of combat. O'Brien knew he was beaten. Over a radio whose batteries were fading rapidly he ordered what was left of the 'Lost Battalion' to make a last desperate effort to break out. At half-past three the survivors radioed back: 'We're coming out. Give us everything you've got!'[4]

Firing every weapon that still could be fired, the unwounded and lightly wounded men of the 'Lost Battalion' tried to make a break for it to the south-west. *Hauptsturmführer* Degen's SS men were waiting for them. Company K, what was left of it, ran straight into the German machine guns and were mown down mercilessly. One hour after they had signalled they were going to break out, K radioed that it was impossible to break through the enemy cordon surrounding the ridge on which they lay.

There were now only 125 fit men left of the 600-odd who had been trapped on the height over a week before. In a last message to them before radio communications broke down and the 157th withdrew, 'abandoning them to the mercy of the enemy' (as the 157th's history puts it), O'Brien ordered the survivors to break up and infiltrate back to the Division's lines. Only two men made it.

Even the hard-bitten veterans of the SS were impressed, as they rounded up the survivors of Companies K, L, I, C and G of the 'Lost Battalion' at five o'clock that afternoon. They found, according to the divisional history of the Sixth SS, *Kampf unter dem Nordlicht*: '456 enlisted men and 26 officers of the 45th Division, most of them wounded. Over two hundred dead were found and buried. Our own losses were 26 dead, 127 wounded and twelve reported missing.'[5] The Battle of the Lost Battalion was over.

Back at the HQ of the withdrawing 157th Infantry Division, the lone two survivors, both soon to be evacuated due to nervous exhaustion, told their tales of what it had been like up there on the ridge, surrounded by the SS. One of them, Pfc Benjamin Melton, said, 'We attacked toward the rear trying to break through. . . . Ammunition was scarce, but we made progress until the enemy artillery zeroed in and some of the men were blown to bits. I saw one officer get a direct hit and just disappear. I was knocked to the ground several times . . . but I wasn't wounded. We saw that we weren't going to be able to get out so we went back to our holes where at least we had a little protection. Somehow the Germans sent word to us to surrender by seventeen hundred hours. But I remembered reading about the massacre at Malmédy* and I didn't want to stay there and be killed in cold blood. Together with Private Walter Bruce and another fellow whose name I don't remember, I set out to try to get back to our lines. . . . We kept halfway up the slopes of the hills and stayed away from all paths and trails. We saw some shoepaks' marks in the snow and followed these for a while. Then we saw a shelter half of which covered a foxhole. We laid low until a GI looked from beneath it. You can imagine just how glad we were to see that.'[6]

---

*See C. Whiting, *Massacre at Malmédy,* for further details.

The other survivor reported how the others had stuck white handkerchiefs around their rifles while the tankers had done the same to the muzzles of their cannon. Then they had placed their rifles muzzle first into the snow to signify they would fire no more. 'We tried to get more of the fellows to go with us, but they were too scared to leave their holes. Being up on that ridge for a week was living hell. It was pretty cold all the time and we didn't get much sleep. We had nothing to eat the last three or four days. The mortar and artillery fire kept us pinned down most of the time and most of the men were wounded from it, especially toward the end when it was thickest. . . . The Germans attacked in strong numbers. They were being mowed down with the help of our artillery, but they still kept coming.'[7]

What was left of the 157th Regiment trailed back the way it had advanced so confidently in what now seemed another age. They had lost over thirty-five percent of their effectives and in the next three days would absorb 1,000 replacements, including fifty officers. Altogether the 45th Division had lost ninety-seven officers and 1,599 enlisted men, a tremendous blood-letting, the like of which the Division had not experienced since the bad days in Italy the year before. As the regimental history of the 157th Infantry puts it bluntly, 'January 21 brought defeat. The Regiment was ordered off the line, leaving behind six of its companies, cut off, surrounded, hopelessly outnumbered. In the mountains the snow deepened.'[8]

On the same day that the 45th Infantry Division received its orders to begin withdrawing to the Moder River line, two men of the 103rd Division staggered into their own lines, naked and stiff and blue with cold. They told the aidmen who tried to revive them that they had been captured by the Germans, who had stripped them of their clothes and then freed them.

At first the men of the 103rd were puzzled by the strange event, but soon they realized what the enemy was up to when more and more Germans dressed as Americans began to probe their positions. As the history of the 103rd Division noted: 'Just before the move the people of Alsace became strangely quiet. The shining joy was gone from the eyes of this liberated people. . . . Tears welled in the eyes of young and old. Alsatians who had given up half or all of their homes to the Cactus (the divisional patch of the 103rd) asked hopefully, "*Vous nix parti?*" Most of the 103rd soldiers, unwilling to break that news and under orders to say nothing, lied in reply. "No, no", they said, "just shifting troops".[9]

But the civilians seemed to know what was going on. Those who had served with the Resistance told the GIs it would be death for them and their families if the Germans returned. The GIs were angry. 'Why pull back?' they asked. 'Why leave these people to the mercy of the SS? Besides, won't we have to take back all this hard-won ground in the spring?' But it was no use. Orders had to be obeyed. Like thieves in the night the Americans began to withdraw that Saturday afternoon, hampered by Germans dressed in American uniform, so that nobody trusted anyone. It was recorded in the 103rd lines that 'the children, always a barometer of native feeling, began to hurl icy snowballs at the troops. The soldiers didn't care much. "We deserve it," they thought.'[10]

It was no different in the villages which had been fought for so hard by the men of the 70th Infantry Division and which now had to be abandoned. Jean Beck, then a youngster in the village of Niederbronn, today a professor at the University of Arizona, recalled: 'Until 20 January it was pretty quiet in Niederbronn. The Americans retreated south-east in the direction of Pfaffenhoffen. All Sunday long there was not one soldier left in the town. However, during the night we heard shooting. On Monday at about 10 a.m. the Germans came from Philippsbourg. In front were a few cars pulled by horses, the Germans being out of gas. Then came a cannon pulled by horses. Everybody else was on foot. We could not understand why the Americans had retreated.'[11]

Thirty years later those bitter memories still lingered. A group of veterans attempting to visit the iron foundry in Niederbronn where they had been billeted in 1945 were turned away in 1979. The factory guard 'explained his uncooperative attitude in a scolding about the January 1945 American abandonment of Niederbronn.'[12]

Some units evacuated the civilian population of the villages they had held to save them from reprisals. Thus the Hellcats' military police company evacuated the civilians at Rohrwiller under fire and were the last to leave the area, save for the final skirmish line.

Others were more concerned with their own safety. The men of the 14th Armored were halted by 155mm cannon skidding off the *pavé* and blocking the road so that the traffic piled up for miles behind it. Now the freezing soldiers sat in their vehicles and thought, 'If the Krauts attack now!'[13] But the Germans didn't attack and they passed through an empty Hatten, cows and pigs poking around in the desolation, looking for fodder.

'There was relief, but not real relief,' as their *Divisional History* records: 'Behind were their friends and comrades, in the rubble of those towns and on those fields, and more of their friends and comrades were in the hospitals. . . . They felt a little as if they were giving up, as if they had fought and suffered and died in vain. . . . And it was a bitter grating night, that night, a night of tears in the soul and it snowed.'[14]

Some didn't get away as easily as Sixth Corps HQ thought they would. The men of the 42nd Division's 222nd Regiment had hardly started to move out at seven-thirty that Saturday evening when the Germans burst right through their final skirmish line. Hurriedly they tumbled out of their trucks and went into action, driving the Germans back into the night. Thereafter they left a retaining force of a squad from each company with orders to make as much noise as possible in order to create the impression that the Rainbow Division was still in the line. The rest stole away in a raging blizzard which wiped out their tracks as if they had never been there.

'For the sake of propriety and then for the salvation of what the Japanese call "Face",' the historian of the 222nd Regiment wrote after the war, 'it was a withdrawal. But in the minds and consciences of the men it was a retreat.'[15]

'It was cold that night, a bitter cold that ate into our bones. It snowed that night, a blinding blanket which wet us to the skin. We retreated that night, a retreat that hurt our minds. But worse than all these things was what our eyes told our soul. Our eyes saw people, newly liberated French people, trudging down those snowbound roads with their houses on their backs and despair in their eyes. Hordes of civilians who had trusted us, moving once again to escape the imminence of a German advance.'[16]

Despite the snow and the icy roads the withdrawal of Brooks' Sixth Corps to the new line of the River Moder was a success. By dusk on 21 January his divisions were well established and substantial reserves had been assembled to meet the expected continuation of the German efforts to retake Alsace. On this new line Brooks had employed the 45th and 103rd Divisions, the 79th with Task Force Linden (42nd Division) attached, the French 3rd Algerian Division, and his only fresh outfit, the veteran 36th Infantry Division. Opposing him from west to east on the same line were 6th SS Mountain Division, the 47th Volks-Grenadier, 7th Parachute, 10th SS Panzer and 21st Panzer

Divisions. The 553rd Volks-grenadier Division was still located in what had been the Gambsheim bridgehead area.

But as the twenty-first came to an end the only American division of Brooks' Sixth Corps actually in contact with the enemy was the 36th Infantry, as the Germans probed for a weak spot in the new line through which to send their armour. They weren't very successful – fifteen German tanks attempting a breakthrough south of Bischwiller were soon knocked out by the Texans' tank destroyers and artillery and a hundred enemy infantry trying to infiltrate their line near Kurtzenhausen were surrounded and mopped up.

That day the Germans contented themselves with following up after the withdrawing Americans, moving up fresh supplies, in particular ammunition. For the German High Command had already ordered the offensive to be continued. The new objective would be Saverne and a fresh attempt made to link up with the German Nineteenth Army attacking northwards from the Colmar Pocket.

So the survivors waited in their new positions for the Germans to come again and once more the snow began to fall.

But at last things were beginning to turn in the Americans' favour. Up in the Ardennes five days earlier, on 16 January, the American northern and southern thrusts into the 'Bulge' had linked up at the Belgian town of Houffalize. Admittedly most of the German troops in the Bulge had managed to escape but the American line was restored and it could be only a matter of time before the Americans attacked once more and reached the positions on the German frontier from which they had been so rudely ejected nearly six weeks before.

On the same day that Patch had given the order for Brooks' Sixth Corps to withdraw to the line of the Moder, the first Russian tanks had crossed the old Polish-German frontier. Now a new threat in the East loomed up for the German High Command, which would soon mean moving the Sixth SS Panzer Army from the Ardennes to meet the challenge. In the Ardennes, therefore, the Germans were now definitely on the defensive which meant that Eisenhower could begin moving troops from that area in order to start clearing up the 'Alsatian sore', which had been troubling him for so long. As early as 18 January he had ordered that the 101st Airborne Division should be moved from Bastogne to take their place in the line with Brooks' Sixth Corps. Soon Eisenhower would move a whole US Corps to Alsace. His aim was to ensure that 'King Jean' would have enough strength finally to eradicate the Colmar Pocket which had been a thorn in his side ever since it had been created, by what Eisenhower believed was a lack of spirit and aggression on the part of the French.

Three days after the withdrawal to the Moder Line, Eisenhower met General Juin once again. Three days earlier de Lattre had counter-attacked against the Germans attempting to break out of the Colmar Pocket, but without success. The weather had been in league with the enemy. The snow was knee-deep and progress would have been painfully slow even without other obstacles; but other obstacles were plentiful – mines, dug-in 88mm cannon, last-ditch-stand machine-gunners, sudden vicious counterattacks. Even the veteran 3rd US Infantry Division, fighting with the French, could make little progress. After forcing their way across the River Ill, the infantry called up the Shermans, only to gaze in horror as the bridge they had captured collapsed under the weight of the thirty-ton tank. The attack came to a standstill.

Thus it was that Eisenhower tried to put some fire into the French. Juin was horrified. As always *la gloire de France* was uppermost in his mind. He reported what Eisenhower had said to de Gaulle and the latter expressed surprise at the 'severity of a judgement' he believed was directed at the French Command and Army. The next day Juin was sent back to Versailles to protest to Eisenhower. The Frenchman reminded him that although the front of the French First Army had been doubled since New Year's Day, it had not lost any ground. Indeed it had just started an offensive, in spite of enormous difficulties. Maliciously Juin added that it was difficult not to make a comparison 'between the valiant efforts they furnish and the goings-on in the neighbouring Army further to the north.'[17] The dig was obvious. The French had stood and slogged it out; the Americans had retreated!

Having made his dig, Juin hurried to reassure the Supreme Commander that 'if errors have been committed . . . the fact remains, nevertheless, that the important thing today is that you win the battle of Alsace as you have won the battle of the Ardennes. That, in my opinion, as I told you yesterday, should be your sole preoccupation of the moment.'[18]

As always Eisenhower backed off when anyone talked tough to him. After all, he saw it as his job to try and hold the alliance together. He told Juin that he had never 'compared unfavourably the troops and leaders of one nationality with respect to any other.'[19]

The next day Eisenhower saw de Gaulle and told him he had no intention of criticizing the French First Army. All he wanted them to do was to clear the Colmar Pocket with the same élan they had shown in Italy and the drive from the beaches. De Gaulle wasn't flattered. He had no intention of frittering away French manpower in what was basically a side-show. The French Army would be needed in full strength for the battles to come in Germany. As always de Gaulle was inclined to let the Americans win his victories for him, if they did not involve French prestige. He pleaded that his First French Army was too weak in infantry and artillery to undertake more than just local actions in the near future. With that Eisenhower had to be content, the problem of the Colmar Pocket still unsolved. He expressed his appreciation for this 'frank exchange of views on little problems that seemed at the moment to be difficult', but which in the end would 'always lead to a mutually satisfactory understanding'.[20]

Understandably 'King Jean' was not a very happy man when he drove to attend the conference at the 3rd US Infantry Division's command post at the small Alsatian town of Ribeauville on 24 January. His forces had been stalled everywhere and 'a certain pessimism hung over the conference'. He listened to his divisional commanders present their 'balance sheets' and then he turned to General Barr, Devers' Chief-of-Staff. 'You can see,' he told the American, 'we cannot extricate ourselves without additional means. So give me the 21st Corps (American) which has nothing to do on the Sarreguemines side. Then you will see.'[21]

Barr smiled in his usual friendly manner, but said nothing. He let 'King Jean' get on with his attempts to cheer up his crestfallen divisional commanders and give them their orders for the following day. When 'King Jean' was finished Barr spoke for the first time. 'If we agree to your request, General, when will the business be finished?' King Jean consulted his map for a moment. 'On 10 February at the latest,' he announced. (he would be one day out). 'Good,' Barr said and that was all.[22]

Six hours later, back at his command post at Rothau, 'King Jean' received a telegram from Devers which read: 'The 21st US Army Corps with its organic elements and the reinforced 75th U.S.I.D will be put under the orders of the French 1st Army immediately. The French 1st Army will place the 3rd and 28th U.S.I.D under the orders of the US 21st Army Corps. . . . General Milburn, commanding the US 21st

Army Corps will . . . report to the General commanding the French 1st Army at Schirmeck at 10.00 in the 25th January'.[23]

Although it was half-three in the morning, 'King Jean' was beside himself with joy. 'God be praised,' he wrote later. 'Now we should have them! . . . With its three army corps, the French 1st Army had victory in its grasp.'[24]

THREE

The long-anticipated attack on the new Moder Line came on the night of 24/25 January as six German divisions struck across the river in three prongs. The worst hit was 42nd Division's 222nd Regiment, guarding a tremendous front of 7500 yards (normally a division would have been used to hold a front line of this length). Standing in their foxholes, some of them knee-deep in water, the men waited tensely that night, for Intelligence had warned them the Germans were going to attack. What Intelligence didn't know was that the 3000-odd men of the 222nd were going to be hit by elements of *five* German regiments drawn from *three* divisions, one of them the 25th Panzer Division.

At six o'clock that night the enemy guns opened up, running a creeping barrage along the American positions in the river valley that ran between Neubourg and Schweighausen. For one hour the guns plastered the 222nd's line; then suddenly they fell silent.

'We waited,' the *Regimental History* recorded, 'Sweat. THEN! All bammed and clattered, streaked and crashed around us until 2000. Shapeless blobs started to poke up out of their positions, moved around and started towards. ONRUSH! Spit on your muzzle, sweetheart, here comes the devil!'[1]

The first wave of German troops easily forded the shallow Moder. They struck the Regiment's positions at Schweighausen, Neubourg and in the Ohlungen Forest. Desperately the defenders sprayed the ranks of the advancing Germans, their bodies outlined a stark black against the lurid unreal light of the blood-red flares. Still they came on, 'half drunk, spurred on by desperate and guttural commands'.[2]

Here and there the Germans broke off the fight, although superiority of numbers was on their side. But as the 24th gave way to the

25th they forced a gap between E and K Companies and immediately started to pour troops into the gap, swinging round behind the American positions. The 222nd's E Company was completely surrounded and cut off. Still it continued to fight on.

Communications from front to the rear began to break down and the harassed battalion commanders could only guess what was happening to their companies. In the end the companies made their own decisions. What was left of E Company fought its way through the Germans and joined K and F Companies which had withdrawn to form a new defensive line. They fought all night and well into the next day until they were exhausted and it became 'an effort to squeeze a trigger or to move, either forward or backward'. In the end the 222nd Regiment stopped the German attack in their sector and as the regimental history records, proved 'something to ourselves: 1. War is hell. 2. We were no longer green. 3. Americans could fight with a cold passion and fury even without that unlimited supply of material which so many believe is responsible for American success in battle.'³

The 222nd men were not the only ones who could claim a success in this new battle. That night the men of the 103rd Infantry Division, dug in between Bischoltz and Muhlhausen, were attacked by a battalion of the Sixth SS Mountain Division 'yelling, cursing in English, scream-ing like madmen'.⁴ The Germans' Intelligence was good. They knew exactly where every important American installation was located. They hit the message centre and the local battalion command post. Communications went. The Americans' main line of resistance was broken. Now something akin to panic broke out. Lieutenant Leonard Doggett scraped together an emergency squad. He threw it into the confused battle around the battalion aid station, fighting off the SS until the wounded and medics could be evacuated. One of this squad was 'a happy-go-lucky kid' named Dennis Bellmore. He and four other men were ordered to guard the crossroads with a light machine gun. The Germans rushed them, but their gun jammed. It was frozen solid. The SS were less than forty yards away. The other four turned to make a run for it, but not Bellmore. The sergeant in charge spotted him on his knees in the snow, his pistol raised.

'What's the matter, kid?' he asked.

'I'm hit,' Bellmore said. 'You guys take off!'⁵

There was not time for arguments. The Germans were almost on to them. The other four ran for safety towards the aid station. As they ran, they could hear the regular spaced-out shots from a .45 pistol, followed by the answering chatter of German burp guns. One last shot and then silence. Dennis Bellmore 'had paid with his life for ten minutes of time . . . precious time during which the aid station and the remainder of the Americans safely left the village'.[6]

There were grimly humorous moments, too, in the fighting on the banks of the Moder that night. In Schillersdorf, which was hastily evacuated just before dawn, three men of the 103rd, not dreaming that they were being attacked by a whole battalion of SS men, decided to 'outflank' the enemy. In the lead, Texan Pfc M. Jacobs bumped into an SS man. The German was too slow on the draw. Jacobs fired first and the German fell into the snow. Now, aware suddenly of their danger, the three ran into a courtyard. Jacobs spotted a door to the street and tried to open it. Suddenly he heard cursing in German on the other side. An SS man was trying to open it too! Jacobs fled. He hid under a wagon and the other two in an outhouse. While the SS questioned the civilians as to the whereabouts of the Americans, a mongrel came up and started to lick the Texan's face. Later the three Americans hid in the attic of a building in which the SS then set up their command post. But after two harrowing days the three were at last rescued.

On the morning of 25 January, the Sixth Corps' line was under attack everywhere. The Germans brought up reinforcements and for the first time in the ETO American troops faced up to attacks by German ski troops, who succeeded in penetrating the village of Muhlhausen.

General Brooks threw in his sole remaining armour, that of the 14th Armored Division. Its 68th Armored Infantry Battalion, supported by tanks of the 25th Tank Battalion, counterattacked in the 222nd Infantry's sector. But although the weary men of the 14th Armored were prepared for another slogging match of the kind they had experienced in the Hatten-Rittershoffen salient, they were in for a surprise. Admittedly here and there the Germans fought to the end and their jet dive-bombers were as active as ever; but the fanatical resistance they had encountered the previous week was absent. They made steady progress without too many casualties, fighting the terrain and the weather as much as the enemy. By that evening they had restored the main line of resistance on the Moder and were actually allowed to leave the front and hold a memorial service for their dead.

Indeed, although a prisoner captured that day declared that the new offensive was intended to capture Strasbourg which would be 'offered to the Führer as a present on 30 January' (the twelfth anniversary of his seizure of power in 1933), Hitler had already commanded that the attack against the Lower Vosges and in Lower Alsace be suspended because the forces being used to attack the Moder Line 'were needed as reserves behind future defensive efforts'.[7]

There would still be fierce local attacks along the Moder Line, but, in essence, the Germans had shot their bolt in France. Now it was up to the Americans to make the running. It was time for them to wipe out the Colmar Pocket. But before that could be done, Eisenhower had to carry out an administrative chore that was to become his most controversial decision of the Second World War, of a kind not carried out by an American commander since the Civil War ended in 1865. The Supreme Commander was to have one of his soldiers shot for desertion.

The young men who fought in Eisenhower's armies were no saints. They led short, brutal lives, at least if they were in the infantry. Junior officers in combat survived, on average, six weeks. Enlisted men could expect twice that long before they were killed, wounded, or evacuated due to illness. When they were lucky enough to get a furlough to 'Pig Alley' (*Place Pigalle*) in Paris or the Rue Neuve in Brussels, their wants were simple – 'booze and dames'. 'The feather merchants' and the 'canteen commandos' of COMZ – 'one man in the line and five men to bring up the Coca-Cola' – might well provide them with movies, USO shows and pretty Red Cross girls serving coffee and doughnuts. But that kind of fare could not help them to forget the horrors they had undergone and which undoubtedly they would soon have to return to, once their 'forty-eight' or 'seventy-two' was over.

In the event some of them lost their nerve and simply didn't go back when the time came – they 'went over the hill'. By December, 1944, there were an estimated 17,000 US deserters in Paris alone, living off their wits, by robbery and the French black market. In virtually every big European city behind the lines, where there were willing whores and B-girls to shelter a soldier, Americans 'took a dive'.

And it was not only when they went on leave. In that winter of 1944/45, with the Germans attacking all the time and the war seeming to go on for ever, an infantry commander might go up into his front at night expecting to find a hundred men manning the line only to discover that half that number remained. The others had simply walked away. There was an epidemic of 'section eight' and 'combat fatigue'. Men made pacts to shoot off each other's big toes, shielding the muzzles of their M-1s with loaves so that there would not be the tell-tale black powder burn of a self-inflicted wound. Older men threw away their false teeth; a man who can't eat, can't fight. Others exposed their feet to the elements in order to get those nice pinky, pulpy toes which indicated 'trench foot'. Some rubbed diesel oil into their chest to produce an incurable itching eczema.

Divisional commanders swore at psychiatrists and in every stockade of every fighting regiment there would be a score of men who would soldier no more, seeking a court martial and a prison sentence as a sure means of evading combat. As we have seen, even when Eisenhower offered in December to erase the sentences of men accused of desertion if they would return to the front and fight again, only a score or so out of the many thousands in confinement took him up on his offer.

Now with thousands of American soldiers on the run all over Europe – one sergeant of the 28th Infantry Division managed to desert from the front line that winter and make his way back all the way to the States! – Eisenhower was faced with a dilemma. His rifle companies were down by ten percent and there weren't enough infantry replacements coming across from the United States to make up the deficiency. Combat fatigue was on the increase and making the gap even bigger. How was he to clear the Colmar Pocket and then launch his armies against what would probably be fanatical resistance in the Third Reich itself?

The infamous 'Massacre at Malmédy', immediately and well-publicized by the Army and the media, back in December, 1944, had helped to steel the resolve of the fighting soldier in the Ardennes. 'Was it any use surrendering to the Germans?', was the message that the Supreme Commander had managed to get across to his soldiers. If you did, they simply slaughtered you in cold blood. It was better just to keep on fighting, even if it was to the death.

What measures, he must have asked himself that January, could he take to combat the rising desertion rate and the lack of will to fight in some of his rifle companies, especially those which were now largely made up of replacements, who knew they were more likely to be killed in their first action than the 'old heads', who stuck together and looked after one another in combat?

On 25 January, 1945, the same day that the Germans made their all-out attack on the Moder Line, Eisenhower made up his mind. Out of the forty thousand deserters apprehended by the military police, of whom 2864 had been tried and sentenced to anything from twenty years to death, he must pick one man and make an example of him. Of the forty-nine American soldiers currently waiting for their death sentence for desertion to be carried out, he picked one man: Private Eddie Slovik of the 28th Infantry Division.

In November, 1944, the 28th Infantry Division had been fighting a desperate battle in what became known as the 'Green Hell of the Hürtgen'. There in the forest which straddles Germany's border with Belgium, the Division had lost 248 officers and 5452 enlisted men. Reinforcements were rushed in in such large numbers that it was impossible to reorganize the badly hit infantry battalions. On 8 November, for example, 515 replacements were integrated into the 2nd Battalion, 112th Infantry, more than half the original strength of the battalion. Companies refused to go into action. At least two battalion commanders were relieved for the same offence. Once it was thought that even a regimental commander was deserting his regiment when he was spotted by the commanding general, General Norman 'Dutch' Cota, wandering around behind the lines (in fact he had just been wounded twice).

It was not surprising, against this background, that General Cota, the hero of Omaha Beach, who had himself been twice wounded in combat, sentenced Eddie Slovik to death for desertion. Not only had this frail soldier, who had served time for petty crimes before the war, deserted in France, he had also refused an unofficial deal just before his court martial. If he would go into the line with his regiment, the 109th, all charges against him would be dropped. He refused and on 11 November, Armistice Day, 1944, the court of the 28th Division, convened by General Cota, sentenced him to death. General Eisenhower confirmed the sentence of death on Private Slovik on 23 December 1944, when the Battle of the Bulge was at its height and the Americans were reeling under the impact of the German attack. One month later the Supreme Commander ordered that the death sentence should now be carried out in the 'regimental area' of the 28th's 109th Regiment from which Slovik had deserted. Two days later, on 25 January, 1945 when General Cota received that order, the 109th's 'regimental area' was in the grimy Alsatian mining town of St Marie-aux-Mines, not unlike Scranton, Pennsylvania, where the 109th had been raised. For in the last week of that January the 28th Infantry Division, newly moved from the Ardennes, formed part of General Milburn's 21st Corps, 'borrowed' by 'King Jean' for the coming assault into the Colmar Pocket. As a warning to the thousands of young replacements who now filled the ranks of the 'Bloody Bucket' Division, as it called itself, (during the Battle of the Bulge the Division had again suffered severe casualties, one of its regiments being practically wiped out), the execution of Private Slovik could not have come at a more timely moment.

On the night of 30 January a snowstorm raged throughout Alsace, but in his château at St Marie, General Frank 'Shrimp' Milburn noticed little of the heavy snow. The undersized Corps Commander, hence the nickname, was nice and snug in the big 18th-century house, which was his Corps HQ. That night he gave a dinner for his divisional generals, with no less a person than Army Group Commander General Devers as guest of honour. The food was good. There was wine and the talk was expansive and confident. Soon the Americans would show the French just how to get rid of the last Germans on French soil!

Near the end of dinner Milburn turned to the head chaplain of 21st Corps, Colonel Edward Elson, who one day would number President Eisenhower among his congregation at Washington's National Presbyterian Church. 'Chaplain,' he said, 'tomorrow morning the 28th Division is going to execute a private soldier by firing squad for desertion. I wish you to attend as my representative and give me a full report.'[8]

The Chaplain acknowledged the order and the dinner continued to the accompaniment of the hearty laughter of successful, well-fed officers, who knew, for the most part, that their lives would not end violently. Indeed, all of them present that night would die in bed, including Colonel Henry Cabot Lodge, liaison officer to 'King Jean', the last to die in 1985. While the generals ate, a weapons carrier that had made the long journey from the US Army's Paris stockade stopped outside a farmhouse which had been commandeered by the Army. Two of the four MPs in the vehicle got out and went into the farmhouse for coffee and food. A little while later, refreshed and warmed, they returned to relieve the other two. Only the fifth man didn't get out. He couldn't, for he sat on the back seat in handcuffs and with his ankles bound!

The first two 'white mice', as the French called them on account of their white-painted helmets, brought the prisoner sandwiches and a mug of coffee. They unlocked Eddie Slovik's handcuffs so that he could eat. But the prisoner was not hungry. He toyed with the food and said, 'Come on fellows, give me a break. Untie my feet and let me run out there in the snow. You can shoot me with your carbines and get it over with.'

One of them shook his head. 'No Eddie, you're a good guy, but we can't do that. They got a big party planned for you over there in St Marie. The full dress treatment. After they get through with you, these dogfaces are supposed to think twice before they take off. Just relax and drink your coffee. It won't be long.'[9]

In his well-known account of what happened to the only American to be shot for desertion in the Second World War, *The Execution of Private Slovik*, written in 1952, seven years after the event, William B. Huie uses the contrasting scenes of the hearty, well-fed Top Brass, warm and jolly in their château, and the skinny little man, bound hand and foot in the truck, pleading to be shot. The reader is expected to have sympathy for Eddie Slovik, who believed he was being executed because once he 'stole a loaf of bread'. (This sent him to reform school, gave him a criminal record, and so he felt, prejudiced General Eisenhower against him.)

Yet, although there is the shock caused by the realization that of the ten million men who served in the US Armed Forces in the Second World War, only one man was executed, the thought also comes to mind that many other young men were prepared to sacrifice their lives for their country, whatever their private fears and wishes: 'the happy-go-lucky kid' Dennis Bellmore; Lieutenant Mahon with his wife and two children waiting for him back in the States; and the rest of the seven-thousand-odd Americans who had been already killed in Alsace alone. They had not run away or thrown away their weapons.

But if he had been a coward in life, Private Eddie Slovik died, it seems, bravely enough. At ten-thirty on the morning of 31 January, 1945, he was taken out into the courtyard of 86 Rue de General Dourgeois,* where, in the presence of General Cota and a firing squad made up of men from the 109th Infantry Regiment, the charges against him were read and he received the General Absolution from a Catholic priest. Then he was led forward to the firing post and his hands were tied. As he was tying Slovik's bonds, Sergeant McKendrick said: 'Take it easy, Eddie. Try to make it easy on yourself and for us.'

Slovik looked at him calmly and said, I'm okay. They're not shooting me for deserting the United States Army. Thousands of guys have

---

* The villa has since been demolished and an apartment block built on the site; even the street name has been changed.

done that. They just need to make an example out of somebody and I'm it because I'm an ex-con. I used to steal things when I was a kid and that's what they're shooting me for. They're shooting me for the bread and chewing gum I stole when I was twelve years old.'[10]

One firing-squad member, Private Morrison, recalled afterwards how, the night before, the twelve men assigned to kill Slovik had discussed the business ahead of them. Most of the men hated the job, but one man said, 'I got no sympathy for the sonofabitch! He deserted us, didn't he? He didn't give a damn how many of us got the hell shot out of us, why should we care about him? *I'll shoot his goddam heart out!*'[11]

Morrison silently agreed with the man. Now, as they lined up their weapons on Slovik, Morrison 'watched him closely for any sign of emotion, but brother, there was none. He was standing there as straight as could be.'[12]

A few minutes later it was all over and Father Cummings of the Third Infantry Division, who had confessed Eddie Slovik, thought: 'Slovik was the bravest man in the garden that morning.'[13]

Minutes later a top-secret, high-priority message was transmitted to Eisenhower's headquarters. It read: 'Pursuant to GCMO 27 Headquarters ETOUSA 23 Jan 45, Private Eddie D. Slovik, 36896415, formerly Company G, 109th Inf, was shot to death by a firing squad at 1005 hours, 31 Jan 45 at St Marie aux Mines, France. Cota.'[14]

Cota later told Mr Huie: 'During the Second World War I was privileged to lead 36,000 Americans into battle and I saw many of them die for the principles in which we believe. Given the same conditions of those hours, I do not see how I could have acted differently in the Slovik case and remained faithful to my responsibilities.'[15]

Now as the last day of January began to draw to a close in St Marie-aux-Mines, Cota prepared to lead another 15,000 young Americans into a new battle, many of them as raw as Eddie Slovik had been. His order to Eddie's old regiment which was going to kick off the 28th Division's attack was simple and optimistic, as befitted the nature of 'Dutch' Cota. It read: 'WE GO TO COLMAR!'

PART IV

Counterattack!

'Whoever wins the winter, wins the war.'
General F. Wiese

ONE

As the combined Franco-American army made its second attempt to break into the Colmar Pocket, King Jean's long-term opponent, General Wiese, commanding the German 19th Army, against whom the Frenchman had been fighting since August, 1944, issued this message to his officers: 'Mail, leave, Christmas, all that will come back again when the result of the battle has been decided and the enemy has been beaten. What will not return is the chance the winter offers us. . . . Whoever wins the winter, wins the war!'[1]

He was right. The Allies certainly possessed the superiority in armour and airplanes. But this superiority was of little use to them in the terrible weather which lasted throughout the course of the battle. The Alsatian plain through which they would attack, resembled, as de Lattre later described it: 'An immense city of the dead, covered with a thick shroud of snow, from which emerged the skeletons of trees haunted by the croaking clouds of crows. And the sky, low and constantly grey, was only lit by the sinister gleam of fires or the blood-red flashes of gunfire.'[2]

For virtually the whole period of the Allied assault the temperature stayed below twenty under zero and there was three feet of snow, across which raced a freezing wind straight from Siberia. It was the coldest winter in Western Europe within living memory. Under such conditions, tank engines refused to start, artillery lenses froze up, infantrymen succumbed to pneumonia by the hundreds. Anyone who left his nose or ears uncovered for more than an hour or so was liable to get frostbite. Wounded left out in the open were more than likely to freeze to death. As de Lattre commented grimly: 'Anyone with a roof over his head – and that was not the attacker – had a master card in the struggle.'[3]

Yet attack they must. De Monsabert, whose Second Corps had already been fighting for a week, was now ordered to attack again. His first objective was to force a crossing of the Ill River with the First French Motorized Infantry and 3rd US Infantry Divisions. Thereafter the French 5th Armoured Division and a combat team from Leclerc's Second Armoured Division would race from the bridgehead gained by the infantry and seize the crossing points on the next water barrier, the Colmar Canal. Then the mixed force of armour and infantry would head east to capture the ancient fortress of Neuf-Brisach and advance to the Rhine. This, it was hoped, would cut off any attempt by the 19th Army to retreat to the Fatherland, leaving Colmar to 'wither on the vine' and fall into Allied hands.

That was the plan. The Third Division, alerted for battle once again after two and a half years of constant combat over two continents, prepared for the winter war. They painted their armoured vehicles white to merge in with the snow which covered the whole of their front. Mattress covers, sheets, pillowcases – anything that was available or could be stolen in the way of white cloth – was hurriedly turned into what the GIs called 'spook suits'. The veterans fashioned themselves little burners, cans filled with anything that would burn, to warm their hands on. Extra clothing was issued; plenty of candy, too, to give the fighting men energy. Soon the men of the Third would be fording the many streams which criss-crossed the Rhine plain and attempting to sleep in the almost unbearable icy winds which swept down constantly from the snow-capped high Vosges Mountains which bordered the battlefield. Like de Lattre, the Third's Commanding General, 'Iron Mike' O'Daniel, knew that the winter was going to be as much of an enemy as the Germans themselves.

But in spite of the terrible weather, the Third's initial attack progressed well at first. O'Daniel's 7th and 30th Regiments reached all their objectives in spite of heavy fighting and dogged resistance by the Germans, well dug-in in the picturesque hamlets and villages which dotted the plain. Then the trouble started.

The First Battalion of the 254th Regiment began to bog down, forced to ferret out the Germans from dug-in positions in a yard-to-yard advance that was bitterly contested all the way. The Third's *Divisional History* states that the 254th's battle for the villages of Houssen, Riedwihr, Holtzwihr and Wicherschwihr, was 'one of the most bitterly fought engagements and without doubt one of the most important that the Third Division ever encountered'.[4]

The regimental commander ordered up his Third Battalion to assist the hard-pressed First. Still the two battalions, sticking like a single finger deep into enemy-held territory, could not overcome the fanatical German resistance. The 254th's sister regiment, the 30th Infantry, which so far had experienced little resistance, pushed forward into the same area around Holtzwihr, not realizing that its flanks were uncovered. The Germans were not slow, as usual, to make full use of their advantage. Two companies of the 30th were attacked inside the village by ten German tanks and a hundred infantry. The tanks split the Americans into little groups. In twos and threes the tanks rattled back and forth, decimating the men of the 30th.

One after another, the three battalions of the 30th Regiment were hit by the Germans. Unsupported by armour, which had not yet succeeded in crossing the Ill, the old 'Tiger' psychosis, that terrible fear of the hitting power of the sixty-ton tank, struck the Americans. The Third Battalion fell back to the Ill 'badly disorganized', as the *Divisional History* puts it delicately. In fact there was something akin to panic and a little later the 30th's commander, Colonel McGarr, was forced to visit individual foxholes under enemy fire to encourage the badly shaken riflemen. He also had to address 'two hundred men lost from their units, giving them talks of encouragement and making arrangements for their re-equipment and prompt return to their organizations', as the *Regimental History* of the 30th Regiment records.[5]

The 30th's Second Battalion was hit just outside Riedwihr. German SPs, low, squat tank-destroyers equipped with an enormous gun, rattled towards them. Men went down everywhere and there was absolutely no cover. Desperately company commanders ordered their men to withdraw. Others simply fled.

But Sergeant Jack Murphy, in charge of a heavy machine-gun section, ordered the five men with him to withdraw while he, single-handed, tackled a German tank advancing on them. For twenty minutes the brave sergeant continued his one-sided duel with the German. A machine gun against a heavily armoured vehicle toting a 75mm cannon! Finally, however, the tank got within fifty yards and opened up at point-blank range. Sergeant Murphy was awarded the Distinguished Service Cross posthumously.

He was not the only one to fight on to the bitter end. Two young officers, Lieutenants Darwyn Walker and Ross Calver, were last seen advancing on a wood held by enemy infantry and tanks. There was a sudden fire-fight and then silence. Some while later two German tanks scuttled out of the wood. The two officers were never seen again.

Here and there odd groups of the badly beaten 30th Infantry were still clinging on to their positions twenty-four hours later, taking everything the Germans could throw at them. But, in the main, the 30th Regiment was, as the *Divisional History* admits, 'in a bad way'.

An urgent call was sent out for uniforms, weapons and hot food. Right down the line of communication the appeal went until it reached the Division's G-4 (supply): 'Send us dry clothes, rifles and machine guns.'[6]

Straggler posts were set up along all possible routes to the rear of the 30th. Wide-eyed, ashen-cheeked soldiers, some without their weapons, virtually all chilled to the bone by that icy wind straight from Siberia, blundered into the posts manned by white-helmeted MPs. Most of the stragglers submitted without a fight. Others refused to 'soldier on' any more and were arrested. Quickly the former were assured that they were safe at last. The officers attached to each post told them there was no need for any further running. They were behind their own lines, defended by massed armour and a solid front of well-armed infantrymen and machine-gunners, dug in west of the Ill.

A few remained undismayed by the disaster which had struck the 30th Infantry Regiment. Even as they wrung the icy water out of their sodden uniforms, their weapons still at their side, they told the hard-eyed officers and MPs manning the straggler posts: 'Yes sir, we can hold! No goddam Kraut is going to kick hell out of us and get by with it! *We'll* be here in the morning!'[7]

It seems that in the Battle of the Colmar Pocket it was not only the big, 'all-American' type who could stand the terrible winter conditions, and also fight desperately and win through in the end. More than once, when one reads through the citations for bravery in the Battle, one is struck that those who won medals came from poor homes, almost as if their poverty or ethnic origins gave them that little edge over their WASP comrades.

The citation of the Medal of Honor awarded to Pfc José Valdez of the Third's 7th Infantry, who died alone covering the withdrawal of his comrades, for instance: 'He was struck by a bullet which, entering his stomach and passing through his body, emerged from his back.

Overcoming agonizing pain, he regained control of himself and resumed his firing position, delivering a protective screen of bullets until all others of the patrol were safe. By field telephone he called for artillery and mortar fire on the Germans and corrected the range until he had shells falling within fifty yards of his position. For fifteen minutes he refused to be dislodged by more than two hundred of the enemy. Then, seeing the barrage had broken the counterattack, he dragged himself back to his own lines. He later died as a result of his wounds.'[8]

In the Second World War the Seventh Infantry, which prided itself that it had been founded in 1808 and affected the title 'Seventh Light Infantry', was awarded six Medals of Honor, all to enlisted men, three of them posthumously. In the *Regimental History* all those men have their portrait except José Valdez. Why was Valdez omitted? Had the authorities no photograph? Or was it because he was a 'spic' or a 'Tex-Mex', whose bravery had gained for him his country's highest award? We do not know. All we know is that the next man to win the coveted decoration in the Third Infantry Division was similarly from an under-privileged background, only in this case he was, admittedly, a white Anglo-Saxon Protestant; and that helped.

On his eighteenth birthday, the earliest he could enlist, he had been turned down for the marines, then the paratroops. The only branch of the US Services prepared to accept the skinny, baby-faced son of Texan sharecroppers was the infantry, and he was not overjoyed by the fact. In Africa he had to fight hard to get sent up the line. In Italy on his first patrol he shot two Italian officers trying to escape. His officer was furious, but that left him cold, just as the killing did. 'I have shed my first blood. I feel no qualms, no pride, no remorse. There is only a weary indifference that will follow me throughout the war.'[9] In the end the baby-faced soldier killed two hundred and forty enemy soldiers, plagued only by a 'weary indifference'.

Now, just returned from hospital, Lieutenant Audie Murphy of the Third's 15th Regiment was ordered to advance on the woods facing Holtzwihr and dig in. Right from the start things went wrong. The young officer spotted one of his men sitting against a tree crying. Murphy asked him what was wrong. The GI replied, 'I've got the shakes!'

'Have you got something on your mind?' Murphy asked.

'No sir. I just started shaking,' the soldier answered, adding that he hadn't slept in a week.

Murphy concluded that the man was 'battle happy' and left him behind. One of his men commented, 'I know how he feels. Many's a time I've just wanted to sit down and cry about the whole damned mess!'[10]

That afternoon Murphy's company was attacked by German infantry and tanks. Soon, of the 128 men in the company, only forty were still on their feet and Murphy was the sole surviving officer of the original seven. When the last American tank destroyer was hit and knocked out, Murphy knew that they were lost.[11] Still he did not lose his head. Instead he ordered the survivors back and began a one-man battle against the Germans. As two full companies of German infantry, both 125-men strong, advanced on him, firing as they came, 'Lieutenant Murphy did the bravest thing that I had ever seen a man do in combat,' an eye-witness, Lieutenant Weispfenning, an artillery observer, reported later. 'With the Germans only a hundred yards away and still moving up on him, he climbed in to the slowly burning tank destroyer and began firing the .50 caliber machine gun at the Krauts. He was completely exposed and silhouetted against the background of bare trees and snow, with a fire under him that threatened to blow the destroyer to bits if it reached the gasoline and ammunition. Eighty-eight millimetre shells, machine-guns, machine pistol and rifle fire crashed all about him.'[12]

Under the cover of smoke a group of Germans advanced against the lone officer along a ditch. They had got to within thirty yards of Murphy when the smoke drifted away revealing them squatting in the ditch, all twelve of them 'like partridges', as Murphy remembered afterwards. Moments later they were very dead birds.

Murphy's uniform was riddled with shell splinters and smouldering from the burning tank destroyer. Still he held up the Germans, calling to the rear all the time for artillery support. Another eye witness, Sergeant Brawley, recalled afterwards: 'The enemy tanks meanwhile returned because Lieutenant Murphy had held up the supporting infantry. . . . These tanks added their murderous fire to that of the Kraut artillery and small arms fire that showered the Lieutenant's position without stopping. . . . The German infantrymen got within ten yards of the Lieutenant who killed them in the draws, in the meadows, in the woods – wherever he saw them. Though wounded and covered with soot and dirt which must have obscured his vision at times, he held the enemy at bay, killing and wounding thirty-five during the next hour.'[13]

In the end Murphy called up what was left of his company and, refusing to be evacuated, he led them in a strong attack which dislodged the Germans from their positions. Only then did he allow the medics to treat his wound in the field. Again he 'felt nothing. No sense of triumph, no exhilaration at being alive. Even the weariness seems to have passed. Existence has taken on the quality of a dream in which I am detached from all that is present. I hear the shells bursting among the trees, see the dead scattered on the ground. But I do not connect them with anything that particularly concerns me.'[14]

But although he insisted to the end of his life that he had felt nothing in combat, that all the brutality and killing had not affected him, that it had all been part of an infantryman's job, *privately* all was very different. In 1971, just before he died, violently as he had lived, he told a doctor that since the war he had been plagued by nightmares in which he relived his combat experiences and that he was unable to sleep without a loaded German Walther automatic pistol under his pillow. How his waking life was also marked by this preoccupation with his combat experience was suggested by his response to the interviewer's question on how combat soldiers manage to survive a war: 'I don't think they ever do.'[15] The combat soldier always paid the price one way or another, either on the battlefield or later.

General Devers had finally succeeded in convincing Leclerc of the French Second Armoured Division that he should serve under de Lattre in Monsabert's Second Corps. Leclerc hadn't liked the idea one bit for he had little time for Monsabert, whom he regarded as little better than a turncoat who had only gone over to the Allies when the fortunes of war had turned. But Devers had coaxed him into the transfer: 'I told Leclerc if he carried out the orders (he would receive from) Monsabert he would find he had nobody in front of him. I said I had made a personal reconnaissance of the front to ensure this was so. He would therefore be able to make a swift breakthrough and join the 21st Corps of the American Army to serve with the Americans again.'[16]

But the attack into the Colmar Pocket was not as easy as Devers had promised. Just like the other veteran division, the US Third Infantry, Leclerc's tankers found the Germans were tough and well dug-in, prepared to fight to the end. The French infantry who were to cover the tanks' advance were exhausted and lagged behind and the going was terrible. All the roads were covered by heavy snow, with mines in the fields on both sides just waiting for the unwary to roll over them.

Leclerc's attack on the village of Grussenheim, supported by elements of the Foreign Legion, ended in disaster for his Combat Command C. Colonel Putz of the Foreign Legion, plus the chief-of-staff, and Captain Pericquet, Leclerc's liaison officer, were killed by an unlucky shell right at the start of the attack. Ten minutes later two of Leclerc's tanks were knocked out by shell-fire blocking the infantry's route so that the latter had to advance without armour, or so de Lattre recorded later.

However, for their part, Leclerc's tankers later maintained *they* had fought without infantry. As Colonel Chatel, Leclerc's aide, stated after the war. 'The infantry did not follow our tanks so that after the armour had taken their objectives, there was no infantry to clean up. The tanks had to stand their ground and were caught among buildings and were hit and destroyed. It was disastrous'.[17]

One of those tankers was Corporal Gaston Fray, whose father was English and who had volunteered for the Second right at the beginning. Now in his tank 'Montmirail', commanded by Lieutenant Louis Michard, a native Alsatian, he found himself in the thick of the battle. Ahead of him he saw another Sherman shudder to a halt, a gleaming hole suddenly gouged in its side. The crew baled out. Two were mown down by the waiting German machine-gunners, 'including a man from Alsace who had thus gone back home to die. I saw another of the original volunteers from my Camberley days killed, a young fellow with an English father like me.'[18]

By now there were only four tanks left in his company. A German tank scuttled through the cemetery to Fray's front, scattering tombstones. A bazooka struck the tank a stunning blow. Snipers opened up from the houses on both sides. Fray could hear the slugs pattering off the Sherman's armour like tropical rain on a tin roof. He knew now 'it was obviously only a matter of time before we would be finished'.[19]

Suddenly he realized that he was not receiving any orders from the tank commander, Lieutenant Michard. As usual he was standing with his head and shoulders boldly exposed in the turret, but he was strangely silent. Fray saw why. He had his head on his arms, with blood trickling down his face. A sniper had shot him. Fray lifted him down behind the cover of a house. There was a 'huge hole at the back of his head and pieces of brain were dropping out'.[20]

Weakly the Lieutenant tried to get up, saying, '*Sauvez moi. Sauvez moi.*'

But there was no saving the Lieutenant who had been with Leclerc ever since the Invasion. He, too, had come home to Alsace to die

That day at Grussenheim the legionnaires lost one hundred and eighty men. But Leclerc's tankers suffered two hundred and seven casualties, including twenty-one officers! Fray's company was typical. It was finished as a unit, with only two tanks left. When one of the company officers, a Captain de Vitasse, saw what had happened, he broke down completely. He had to be removed, suffering from combat fatigue and a broken heart.

The débâcle at Grussenheim was too much for Leclerc, who shortly after visited his decimated Combat Command C there. He sent his aide, Colonel Chatel, to Devers to complain. After being shot at several times by trigger-happy American sentries, the Colonel finally saw the Army Group Commander.

'What is it?' Devers asked curtly. It was not customary for mere colonels to ask to speak to an Army Group Commander personally. Chatel stood his ground and said Leclerc had instructed him to speak privately to him.

'Why is it your General does not want to fight?' demanded Devers.

Chatel flushed. 'My General does not want to fight because he does not want his division to be destroyed in operations which are haphazard and not properly prepared and which cannot possibly succeed because a complete disregard for the rules of deployment of armour is being shown by a man who thinks only in terms of infantry!'

Devers did not seem to be offended by this attack on de Lattre. Instead he said quietly: 'You seem to like your General pretty well. Tell me all then.'

Chatel told him about the Grussenheim battle and 'what a fearful disaster' it had been. The Army Commander followed him with interest. Finally he said, 'Thank you very much for telling me the truth. Tell General Leclerc I will see him tomorrow morning and that I will fix it.'

Chatel, who had thought he 'might have been shot for mutiny', was overwhelmed by such kindness and promised he would inform Leclerc. Back at Second's HQ, Leclerc's lean face broke into a grin when Chatel told him how Devers had remarked that Leclerc didn't seem to want to fight. He told Chatel that it was exactly the same remark that de Gaulle had made to him when he had visited the General to protest against having to fight in the ranks of the First French Army: 'Why is it you do not want to fight?'[21]

Next day Leclerc told Monsabert that he could not clear the woods outside Grussenheim if the unit concerned was not supported by two fresh battalions of infantry. Monsabert said he simply could not provide fresh foot soldiers; the barrel had been scraped clean. Leclerc would have to attack with what he had. Fortunately for him, who might well have faced a court-martial for having virtually refused a direct order, the Germans on Monsabert's front began to withdraw that day, leaving behind only a handful of last-ditch defenders. Hastily General Devers stepped in and Leclerc's division was transferred to General Milburn's 21st Corps, together with O'Daniel's Third Infantry Division. The American Devers had saved Frenchman Leclerc from the wrath of his fellow-countrymen yet once again. One day Devers, and perhaps the whole of the United States, would come to regret it.

TWO

In spite of his difficulties with the insubordinate, rebellious Leclerc, who, through his connections with the Americans, had escaped from the French command yet again, King Jean was pleased. Not only was the German resistance in the Colmar Pocket crumbling at last, but now he had a whole corps of Americans under his personal command. For the first time since France had re-entered the war on the Allied side, the French, in the shape of General de Lattre de Tassigny, could decide the fate of some 100,000 American GIs of General Milburn's 21st Corps.

The little American General had impressed King Jean at their first meeting. De Lattre found the American 'lean and muscular and straight of eye, with the energetic features of a fighter'.[1]

As Monsabert's Second Corps consolidated its gains against the rapidly weakening Germans on its front, de Lattre ordered Milburn to attack towards the fortress of Neuf-Brisach, east of Colmar. He was to capture it before the Germans could establish a firm defence there. Thereafter his Corps was to push on to the River Rhine, and, as de Lattre wrote later, 'if circumstances then proved accommodating, not to hesitate in creating a bridgehead *east* of the river'.[2]

It was an incredibly bold plan. Five weeks before any real attempt was to be made to 'bounce the Rhine', as Montgomery had described the operation so lightly in the days of victory back in September, 1944, here was de Lattre hoping that a single US Corps would be able to force Germany's last great natural bulwark – a task which, in the end, would take whole armies to carry out!

In the event, it was to be another two months before Milburn's Corps crossed the river. For, unknown to de Lattre, the Germans were already preparing to evacuate what was left of the Colmar Pocket and blow the bridges across the Rhine behind them.

Four days before Milburn's Corps began its attack east, the German Commander-in-Chief West had been empowered to 'withdraw the weakly held Ill front to a straight line between the Ill and the Rhine, and *beyond* the Rhine as soon as defences had been erected'.[3]

Work had begun to start a ferry service to augment the flow of traffic eastwards across the bridge at Brisach (in Germany). Work was also going ahead to build three heavy and two light cable tracks across the Rhine. But although the top German generals urged an immediate evacuation of the Pocket, whose maximum width had now been reduced to twenty-five miles, with the Allies only five miles from the vital bridge at Brisach, Hitler refused. On the same day that de Lattre gave Milburn his orders, the Führer refused to sanction the evacuation of the Colmar Pocket. He ordered that the Vosges front to the west should be lightly held, but the units within the Pocket should be deployed to defend the prestige towns of Colmar and Mulhouse. There would be no simple jaunt to the Rhine for Milburn's Corps.

But at first it was easy. At nine o'clock on 2 February the three battalions of Eddie Slovik's old outfit, the 109th Infantry of General Cota's 28th Division, attacked Colmar. Working south along the west bank of the River Ill, the men of the 'Bloody Bucket' division met surprisingly little resistance. They overcame the lone German machine-gunners and groups of last-ditch infantrymen and soon reached their first objective: a line running east to west in the northern outskirts of Colmar. Now, with a combat command of the French Fifth Armoured Division, the 109th began to advance into the city itself. The speed of the Franco-American advance caught the German defenders completely by surprise. It did the local civilians, too.

As one eyewitness reported: 'It was Sunday and all the people were dressed in their best clothes walking down Beethovenstrasse going to church. High in the dirty, misty sky several Messerschmitts were slipping inside the flak, peeling off, diving to bomb the city's outskirts. Shells were zooming so low over the city that you kept wanting to fall flat on your face. Tanks, trucks and troops were rushing through the streets of the city in several directions. And on Beethovenstrasse lying in a sticky pool of blood there was a dead German sniper. But except for a small circle of kids staring at the dead Nazi, the civilians didn't seem to notice him, just as they didn't seem to notice the trucks, nor the tanks nor the shells nor the planes. It was as if they were trying to separate themselves from the war by ignoring it. Or was it just that they had been seeing and hearing war for weeks now and it had become part of them? Now it was Sunday and Colmar was free and they were going to church.'[4]

'Dutch' Cota left the ceremonial capture of the city which had defied all de Lattre's attempts to take it since October, 1944, to the French Fifth Armoured. Mopping up all opposition as they raced through the streets, noting just how lucky they had been – for the city's defences were formidable – the men of the 109th headed for the high ground to the west, south and east. From here they would attack towards the Rhine, together with the 'Hellcats' of the 12th Armored Division, 'still somewhat groggy from its experiences of Herrlisheim, despite the arrival of replacements',[5] as the *Divisional History* put it rather mildly.

But if the Americans were not inclined to celebrate while there was still fighting to be done, the French Army savoured *its* triumph at Colmar. Colonel Scott of the Third Division, hearing that Colmar had just been taken, set out with a fellow officer, Charlie Spreyer, to have a look at the city. But he didn't get far. Just as their jeep emerged from the woods to the north of the city, 'there was a jumbled roar along the road ahead, and a column of jeeps heading our way spewed out on to the snow-covered flat. With complete abandon the jeeps raced across the snow to see which would be first in line on the way back to Strasbourg from Colmar.'[6]

What the amazed Colonel had just seen was a column of excited French war correspondents taking part in a crazy race to reach Strasbourg first and file their stories for the Paris press. *Colmar had fallen!*

Naturally King Jean was overjoyed when he heard the news. Swiftly he wrote two messages that Sunday. One was directed to the citizens of Colmar, German-speaking for the most part and many of them pro-German still, in which he expressed 'the affection of France, the pride of the Army and my own happiness – one of the purest I have ever known'.[7] It read: 'Inhabitants of Colmar! After four and a half years of oppression and suffering, four years and a half of a separation so cruel to our hearts, your city has found the motherland and the tricolour once more. United in brotherhood, the French of the 5th Armoured Division and the infantry of the American divisions have today, 2nd February, entered the city of Colmar, which our manoeuvre has sought to spare from the destruction of battle.'[8]

Having given himself an understandable pat on the back, de Lattre dictated a more practical and down-to-earth message to General Milburn, whose corps had really made it all possible. It read: 'It seems that the Germans, having now decided to evacuate the Alsatian pocket, and abandoning the use of the Brisach bridge for their withdrawal, intend to operate this withdrawal through Chalampé under the protection of the Hardt forest. . . . Thus with the least possible delay and with the maximum strength, the whole mass of the US 21st Army Corps will be launched due south upon the backs of the defenders of the southern front, in the two directions of Ensisheim and Chalampé.'[9]

To do this the 12th US Armored and Leclerc's 2nd Armoured Divisions were to proceed south 'with the greatest urgency'.

As far as the last German fortress on the western bank of the Rhine, Neuf-Brisach, was concerned, de Lattre stated: 'I wish to make it clear that it is simply a matter of being ready to seize every favourable opportunity in this respect, but that the execution of such an operation should not harm the conduct of the vigorous southward exploitation.'[10]

So the Hellcats of the 12th US Armored Division set off for the new battle. They rolled through Colmar, celebrating at last. 'Dead Germans littered the main thoroughfares and the parks were covered with dead men and artillery horses. The French throngs paid no attention to the enemy dead. Some French even stood on the dead bodies in order to get a better view of the passing American armored column!'[11] But the Hellcats had no time to celebrate. There was a battle to be fought and a war to be won, though, as their *Divisional History* records: 'On numerous occasions French forces came up to occupy French towns after Hellcat combat drives had cleared them of Nazis. French commanders apparently took this attitude: "The Americans can go and fight. We will stay and kiss the girls." '[12]

The Third Division's Seventh Infantry Regiment prided itself on being the oldest fighting organization in the United States Army. The 'Cotton Balers', as the Regiment called itself, had begun its fighting career in 1812 in combat against the invading British. Thereafter it had taken part in every major American action and had been one of the first US units to see action in the west when it had attacked on 8 November, 1942 at Fedala, French Morocco. Ironically enough, the

Regiment's first combat experience was also against an ally, for Fedala was defended by the French Army.

Two and a half years later, after four amphibious assaults against hostile shores and having suffered some 10,000 casualties, the Cotton Balers were beginning their last action on French soil. The Regiment was not in a particularly good shape. Only the day before it moved into battle, the regimental surgeon had reported to its commander, Colonel Heintges, that some 200 of his soldiers were suffering from frostbite and would soon succumb to trench foot if they were not taken out of the line. But Heintges would only allow the worst cases to be sent to the rear for treatment. For he was desperately short of men and of a mere eighty replacements sent up for the rifle companies that day, only a handful were adequately equipped for winter warfare. Reluctantly Heintges ordered them not to be assigned to the fighting companies until they were properly kitted out. Still 'torn in mind and body as they were', as the *Regimental History* records somewhat melodramatically, 'but with the determination to uphold the great traditions of the Regiment of overcoming all obstacles, they stuck grimly to their assignments and prepared to smash the enemy once more.'[13]

At five o'clock on the morning of the same day that Colmar was captured, the Seventh Infantry went into the attack between the Rhine-Rhône Canal and the Rhine River itself. Their objective was to seal off the fortunes of Neuf-Brisach which guarded the vital bridge across the Rhine. At first the going was easy. But once the infantry entered the little village of Biesheim to the north of Neuf-Brisach all hell was let loose. In the light of a waning moon, the Americans were ambushed by a large force of Germans who outnumbered them four to one. Here and there the Americans went to ground, as the tracer zipped back and forth frighteningly in the confused street fighting. Others engaged in hand-to-hand combat with a very determined enemy. The situation started to worsen rapidly. T/5 Forrest Peden, an artillery observer with the 10th Field Artillery Battalion, pelted eight hundred yards through a hail of fire to the infantry's CP. He told the battalion commander what was happening up front, his jacket ripped by enemy bullets, his face glazed with sweat. Then he volunteered to guide two light tanks back to help the trapped infantry. Knowing the risk involved, he climbed on to the deck of the lead tank and guided it into the embattled village, where an eerie battle was now taking place between the tombs of the old Jewish cemetery.

Just as the tank reached the ditch where many Americans were trapped, it was struck by a German anti-tank shell. It started to blaze fiercely. But as the crew fled, Peden died on the deck, consumed by a funeral pyre of burning fuel. Yet again another brave man had won the Medal of Honor posthumously.

But Peden's death had not been in vain. The attack was pushed home and the battle of the Jewish cemetery was concluded with the Seventh capturing what was left of it as well as the pillboxes between the cemetery and the Rhine.

Now the Seventh started to send out patrols towards Neuf-Brisach itself. One of them reached within five hundred yards of the walled city, which had been built in 1472. In the eighteenth century Vauban, the famed military engineer who had fortified the whole length of the French frontier for Louis XIV, had built one of his forts at Neuf-Brisach – a low, star-shaped series of walls around the citadel. The patrol returned with twenty-four prisoners and the information that from a distance the place looked like a 'waffle'. Thereafter Neuf-Brisach was known to the GIs, with their habit of always turning something strange and frightening into something more familiar, as 'Waffle City'.

Now the two sister regiments of the Seventh began to concentrate around the last serious obstacle in their advance to the Rhine. While the Seventh worked its way to the north-east of the fortification, which was still a completely unknown quantity to Allied intelligence, the 30th Infantry Regiment moved to the north. For its part, the Third's 15th Infantry advanced cautiously south-east along the bank of the Rhine.

Lieutenant Audie Murphy, in action once more and fearing another ambush of the kind which had been sprung on the Seventh at Biesheim, led his men of the 15th Infantry forward very cautiously. As they approached Neuf-Brisach: 'We creep as stealthily as mice through the strange territory. A brick wall rears up before us. We pause, listening intently for the clink of metal, the guttural whisper, the scrape of a boot. But, except for the sighing of the wind through the trees, there is no sound'.[14]

Murphy rolled over the wall to find himself in a graveyard. The wall extended right round the place and in case of attack, the tombstones would provide cover. He signalled his men forward. Tired and miserable as they were, they couldn't overlook the irony of their situation.

'The graveyard company finally gets home!'

'Move over, friends. You got some company.'

'Be funny to wake up here in the middle of the night.'[15]

Murphy hissed at them to be quiet and get to work. Hastily they knocked holes in the wall for their machine guns before bedding down, Murphy himself guarding the gate.

Twice the tired young officer nodded off, so in the end he took his pistol out of its holster and held it at his waist with both hands. The next time he dozed off the gun slipped from his fingers, struck his feet and brought him back to consciousness.

At dawn his sergeant, Bergman, called him with a whispered, 'This is a set-up right out of the book. Look!'

Murphy peered through a hole in the wall. Directly to his front in an open field a German sergeant was standing stretching and yawning. Obviously he had just woken up. Fascinated, the young officer watched as the German called an order. From the foxholes all around sleepy men in dirty field grey began to rise from their holes like wan ghosts.

Bergman chuckled and lined up his sights. 'Dying at dawn is going to be easy,' he said. 'They can just turn over and go back to sleep – for ever!' Murphy counted the Germans. There were twenty of them.

'You think that's all of them?' Bergman asked.

'Must be. Okay, let 'em have it!'

The machine gun burst into life. Four of them went down immediately in a flurry of whirling arms and legs. Bergman fired another burst. Two more Germans fell. Abruptly the others were shooting up their hands in panic, crying to their unseen assailants, *'nicht schiessen, kamerad, nicht schiessen.'*

'Just like something from the books,' Bergman commented, well pleased with himself.

'Yeah,' Murphy agreed. 'Okay men, go out and get them.' Another day of war had begun.[16]

The noose around 'Waffle City' was pulled ever tighter with the three sister regiments jostling for position and the honour of capturing the last real German stronghold on French soil. On 6 February, elements of the Seventh's 2nd Battalion reported heavy enemy traffic evacuating Neuf-Brisach along the south-east road leading to the Rhine. The Second Battalion was ordered to bring down fire, with every weapon it possessed, on the road.

Patrols were sent out to probe the town's defences, now that the enemy seemed to be evacuating Neuf-Brisach. One reported seeing a white flag hanging over an entrance to 'Waffle City', but others were fired upon. What was going on inside the ancient fortress? The Third Division linked up with the men of the US 75th Infantry Division fighting towards Neuf-Brisach from the south. Now 'Waffle City' was virtually sealed off. How much longer would it hold? And which regiment would be the first to enter it? It could not be much longer now.

After the war General George C. Marshall, the US Army's Chief-of-Staff, wrote in his account of the fighting, 'The Winning of the War in Europe and the Pacific', that 'the climax of the battle was a night assault on the bridgehead town of Neuf-Brisach by infantry of the US Third Division using assault boats and scaling ladders on the moats and walls of the fortified town, very much after the fashion of medieval battles'.

For such a dour man, George Marshall certainly let his imagination have full rein in his description of the battle for Neuf-Brisach. For, in truth, it was broad daylight when the fortress was finally taken. The moat was completely dry and had been for over a century *and there was no assault*.

On the morning of 6 February, 1945, the commanding officer of the Third Division's 30th Regiment told the CO of his First Battalion Lt Colonel Porter, that he wanted a waffle for breakfast. The hint was all too obvious and Colonel Porter had no intention of failing his regimental commander. That morning he sent out a number of patrols towards the squat fortress, its outline distorted by what Vauban had called a 'pregnant wall': a stone wall bolstered by a sloping wall of earth which made it difficult for cannon in time of siege to get within firing distance. It was the task of these patrols to find out at last what was going on in Neuf-Brisach.

The first patrol of the First Battalion, led by Sergeant Tapley, reached the northern end of the town at eight o'clock that morning and was fired upon by a machine gun. It retreated but returned later to find a white flag flying over one of the arched entrances to the eighteenth-century fortress. In the meantime another patrol, led by Sergeant Robert Weiler, reached the town at nine-thirty. Close to the railway bridge the cautious Americans spotted a civilian watching them. In sign language and plenty of broken French, they finally persuaded the Frenchman to lead them into the city. He guided them into the dry moat and the infantrymen followed him through a narrow, low-ceilinged sixty-foot tunnel, dripping with nitre, into Neuf-Brisach. But they weren't the only Americans in the city by now. In the meantime Sergeant Tapley's patrol had also contacted the French in the shape of two shabby, but curious young children. They were happy to jump down into the moat, from whence they led the Americans through an arch into the town.

In the end it was discovered that the Germans had fled from Neuf-Brisach after all, leaving behind them a total of seventy-six men, who drifted in in twos and threes to give themselves up. So it was that at fifteen minutes past eleven that morning Colonel Porter could proudly radio his Regimental Commander that 'Waffle City' had fallen without a single American casualty.

The Third Infantry Division's part in the Battle of the Colmar Pocket was about over. In sixteen days of fighting the Division had won three more Medals of Honor, captured twenty-two towns and taken 4200 prisoners. It had virtually destroyed what was left of the German 708th Volksgrenadier Division and the 2nd Mountain Division. But again the cost had been high. In the Division's Thirtieth Regiment alone, there had been a total of 1170 casualties, one-third of its strength. It was no different in its sister regiment, the Seventh, which claimed that it always suffered more casualties than any other regiment in the US Army. The Seventh also lost one-third of its strength in killed, wounded and missing. Indeed the costs were high for virtually every unit engaged in the last battle. Of the total of 420,000 Allied troops involved, 295,000 French and 125,000 American, the French lost a total of 14,065 men killed, wounded and missing and the Americans 6400.

But the fighting was not over yet. While Major Scott of the 12th US Armored Division shook hands with Colonel Deleuze of the 4th Infantry near the village of Rouffach to symbolize that the Colmar Pocket had been cut in two, de Lattre was considering what he was going to do next.

Of the former Colmar Pocket, the Germans now held only a rectangle, twenty by fifteen miles. Its long sides ran from the River Ill to the village of Logelheim, south-east of Colmar, to Illzach, north of Mulhouse; then along the Rhine from Brisach to Petit Landau. Already Intelligence had informed King Jean that the secondary roads that criss-crossed what was left to the Germans were crowded with panic-stricken Germans attempting to find a crossing over the Rhine.

In particular, the Boche were heading for the villages of Balgau and Blodelsheim and the two bridges at Chalampé. As far as Intelligence could ascertain the crossing points were defended by one German division, which was, however, fighting quite resolutely, especially in the area of Chalampé.

De Lattre ordered the American 21st Corps and the French First Corps under General Bethouart, who had once briefly languished in a Vichy prison because he had plotted with the Americans prior to their invasion of North Africa, to give the Boche the *coup de grâce*. The German 19th Army, which had defied him time and again since the Allied landings in Southern France the previous August, was not to escape him this time.

THREE

'Germany passed its last night in France,' King Jean wrote in February, 1945.[1]* The German 19th Army, what was left of it, held four small villages on French soil: Rumersheim, Bantzenheim, Ottmarsheim and Chalampé. After four and a half years of occupation, France was nearly free. As patrols from his First Army started to probe the German strongpoints on the west bank of the Rhine, de Lattre told himself that the words of the great 18th-century French commander still held true: 'No man of war should rest while there remains a single German on this side of the Rhine.'[2]

But if the end was near for the Germans, the patrols of his Second and Ninth Divisions treated the defeated enemy with care as they circled the first three of the strongpoints, trying to find their weak spots. There were mines everywhere in the mud and melting snow, and the defenders fired at the first sight of any movement. At this stage of the battle, de Lattre's infantry, whose losses in the rifle companies had reached a staggering 35 to 40 percent, were taking no unnecessary risks.

For most of that night the men on patrol could hear the constant roar of traffic fleeing across the bridge at Chalampé, the last German escape route. Then just before dawn the noise ceased and there was a strange echoing silence. What was going on? Were the Huns going to play another dirty trick on them?

The men of the Ninth Infantry crept ever closer to the great last water barrier, tensed for the first burst of enemy machine-gun fire. Were they walking into a trap? Why had the firing ceased so abruptly?

* This was not strictly true. There would be German troops in isolated fortress ports such as Le Harve, Dunkirk and Lorient right to the end of the war.

The breeze coming from the river to their front was warm and balmy, no longer that freezing blast straight from Siberia. It seemed to herald the spring, a sign of hope and renewal. But the weary French infantry stealing through the barren, shell-torn fields, criss-crossed by irrigation ditches, remained hesitant. Yard by yard they approached the bridge at Chalampé.

At eight o'clock that morning the horizon to their front was split by a burst of violet flame, followed by the hollow boom of high explosive. The men of the Ninth Infantry knew what had happened and relaxed at once, knowing that on this day, at least, they would not die. The Boche had blown the last bridge at Chalampé behind them. The Colmar Pocket existed no more. The enemy had fled.

A few minutes later the infantry of the 2nd and 9th French Infantry Divisions reached the banks of the Rhine to see the smoking remains of the Chalampé railway bridge straddling the great river in twisted confusion. As far as the eye could see, there was no field-grey uniform in sight. The enemy had gone to ground in his own country, waiting for the new battle to come – the attack across the Rhine.*

The Allies had lost 18,000 casualties in reducing the Colmar Pocket, but it was calculated that the Germans had suffered 22,000. Of the eight German divisions engaged in the final battle, only one, the 708th Volks-grenadier Division, escaped reasonably intact. The German 19th Army virtually ceased to exist. For the top brass it was a victory. As always on such occasions, they issued grand-sounding victory communiqués. On that day de Lattre, for example, told his triumphant troops: 'On the twenty-first day of a bitter battle during which American and French troops have rivalled one another in enthusiasm, tenacity and manoeuvrability, the enemy has been driven from the Alsatian plain and has been forced back across the Rhine. The Allied forces of the French 1st Army are lining the river throughout its length in their sector. They have kept to the words of Turenne: "No man of war should rest while there remains a single German on this side of the Rhine."'[3]

One day later, on the 10th, General Devers issued his own statement, full of the rhetoric and purple prose beloved by top brass in moments of victory: 'You have freed the imperial city of Colmar, the name of which is scattered through the pages of French history and is dear to the heart of every Frenchman. You have given independence to

---

* See C. Whiting, *Bounce the Rhine*, for further details.

thousands of civilians of a noble land filled with love of liberty.... To the officers and men of the French 1st and 2nd Corps, to the American 21st Army Corps, to the Service departments of these corps and of the army, I say: "Well done! Let us all go forward to our new task more determined than ever to destroy the forces of evil. I say to you: *Forward to Germany.*"[4]

Eisenhower was, naturally, not to be left out of the flood of congratulatory messages which were winging their way back and forth between the triumphant generals. Although only nine days before, he had rated Devers so low in his list of commanders, Eisenhower cabled the Commander of the Sixth Army Group on 9 February: 'I beg you to accept my congratulations ... on the splendid realization of your troops in the liberation of Colmar and the elimination of the enemy's bridgehead west of the Rhine. This victory, achieved in the face of difficulties of weather and terrain, is an exceptional example of the Allied fighting team work.'

In spite of the fact that he thought that 'French divisions are always a questionable asset' and that the 'French continue to be difficult ... I must say that next to the weather I think they have caused me more trouble in this war than any other single factor',[5] Eisenhower ordered Devers 'to transmit to General de Lattre, commanding the French 1st Army, and to all the forces under his command, my congratulations on this great achievement'.[6]

There were parades, parties and decorations handed out by the basketful. Although most of the local menfolk were still fighting stoutly in the *Wehrmacht* on the other side of the Rhine'* de Lattre felt, 'what an outburst of joy there was. At all the windows the plebiscite of flags was triumphant. All the villages stirred themselves to welcome their liberators and, despite the agony of many forced absences, made worse from that moment by complete silence, all the houses were opened to those who had given them their homeland. Never in its fiery history had Alsace known such a fever. Doubtless because it had never suffered nor hoped so much.'[7]

Naturally General de Gaulle was not slow to make political capital out of the victory in order to bolster up his shaky position in France. Although in this week of victory he asked Eisenhower to allow him to

---

* At the time of writing this, the local Alsatian papers headlined the news that Russia had finally admitted that many hundred of Alsatians fighting with the German Army had died in that country long after the war was over, presumably in the forced labour camps of the Gulag.

pull back three of de Lattre's divisions to train new units and 'to assure contact between certain regions of the country and its organized Army'[8] – in other words he was having trouble with the communists of the French resistance once again – de Gaulle hurried to Colmar to take part in the victory parade.

Colmar's Place Rapp, where the Hellcats had seen the French standing on the dead bodies of the defeated Germans to get a better view of the victorious French armour, was hastily cleaned up. French and American flags went up on all sides. The eighteenth-century houses, pocked by shell-fire, were hung with bunting and decorated with spring flowers. The weather had turned very mild and the sun shone fitfully.

The clarions shrilled, the kettledrums rattled, the brass blared, as the crowds cheered wildly. Men straight out of the line, hastily cleaned up and drilled on how to march 'in a soldierly fashion', paraded through the cobbled streets. Speeches were read out. Medals were presented. Every one of the top brass received something. De Gaulle even presented Leclerc with the Cross of the Grand Officer of the Legion of Honour, after de Lattre had received his Grand Cross. Like Napoleon before him, Charles de Gaulle was liberal with shiny baubles. General 'Iron Mike' O'Daniel, who had had his first taste of combat not far from there as a young officer with the 11th Infantry, was made an honorary private first class in the French Foreign Legion.

But for the 'dogfaces', as they called themselves a little wearily, there were few decorations and no celebratory dinner-parties. For them the whole weary business was about to begin yet again.

While the Third Infantry Division rested for a month before beginning its long race across Southern Germany, before the US 101st Airborne and Leclerc's Second Armoured, filling in the gaps left by the 4500 casualties suffered in the last three weeks, Cota's 28th Infantry returned to the front in Germany almost immediately. Once more the 'Bloody Bucket' Division went back to 'Heartbreak Corner' in the 'Green Hell of Hurtgen' where it had suffered so grievously in the bitter fighting of the previous autumn.

General 'Slim' Gavin of the 82nd Airborne, which had taken part in some severe fighting during the Bulge, went up with them. Travelling in his jeep, accompanied only by his driver, he followed the abortive advance the 28th Division had made six months before, to find 'all along the sides of the trail there were many dead bodies, cadavers that had just emerged from the winter snow. Their gangrenous, broken and torn bodies were rigid and grotesque, some of them with arms skywards, seemingly in supplication. . . . As darkness descended upon the canyon, it was an eerie scene, like something from the lower level of Dante's *Inferno*. Some little while later the trim young airborne commander came upon one of his battalions, filled up with replacements, resting in that grim forest. One of his men, he observed, 'began to turn pale, then green, and was obviously about to vomit'.[9]

Even as they celebrated at Colmar and those few of the 103rd Infantry Division fortunate enough to do so watched Ingrid Bergman in *Gaslight* or Jennifer Jones in *The Song of Bernadette* in the crude frontline cinemas set up in barns and local schoolhouses, the fighting in Alsace-Lorraine continued. On the same day that they held the victory parade in Colmar, the US 44th Infantry Division which had been so badly hit on the first day of the offensive, was attempting to retake two fortified farmhouses they had lost. In the course of what was just a local action, they lost over a fifth of an infantry battalion, 145 men killed and wounded.

Not far away the green 70th Infantry Division, which had suffered nearly 3500 casualties in its first taste of combat in January, was also back in the line, fighting in the Saar. Again it suffered heavy casualties.

Typical of those anonymous young men who fought, suffered and died that February while the top brass celebrated *their* victory was the young officer in the 70th Division, whose men called him 'Little Boy Blue'. His real name was Harold D. Wilson. He had failed West Point and had joined the artillery as an enlisted man. But he had always wanted to be a combat soldier and had somehow succeeded in having himself transferred to the infantry. Now he commanded an infantry platoon in the 70th.

'Although he was twenty-one, Wilson looked about seventeen or eighteen,' one of his men wrote in 1945. 'He had blond hair, baby blue eyes and about as much of a beard as yours truly. His voice was high and his enunciation clear. When he intoned "Column right, MARCH" in his high little voice you had to smile and shake your head. He was very precise and GI. He was soon to fall heir to the name of 'Little Boy Blue' and the name fitted him well. I liked him, but the thought of this almost ridiculous little character leading a platoon of men into combat was too much.'[10]

But 'Little Boy Blue' turned out much better than anyone expected in the Division's first taste of combat. He was wounded, but refused to be evacuated. He encouraged and chivvied his men all the time, keeping up their morale, rarely letting them rest, always maintaining, 'We'll keep busy up here if it's doing nothing but melting snow to wash our feet.'[11]

Now he was in a company which marched straight into two German machine guns. One platoon was cut down immediately. Little Boy Blue's own platoon was pinned down by murderous enemy fire and stayed crouched low till dawn when the rumour passed from man to man that they were going to pull out soon.

'The men were on the verge of panic,' wrote Private Kevin Corrigan of his platoon after Little Boy Blue was dead. 'Up stands Wilson and ignores the enemy fire and runs all over the place; gets protection on the flanks and gets the rest of the company and tells them they're going to attack with him. Everything is pretty active with heavy mortar and machine-gun fire, but he's running around to the platoons, shouting "Here, here, you men, where are you going? You come right back here! Over there, Sergeant. Bring those men by you up here. We're going to attack these woods!" His way from the first to the third is barred by a stream of machine-gun fire. He simply hurdles it. He got things organized and by a miracle wasn't killed. He was hit in the face and leg by a Panzerfaust shell, but as usual, if a wound didn't kill him it couldn't stop him. He led the company into a smashing assault which led the division. Do you get the picture? This gentle guy with no fear.'[12]

Three weeks later Little Boy Blue was dead, shot in the head by a sniper, while peering from a window during an attack. He said to the two men with him, 'Now, don't worry. I'll be all right.' He started to fade and asked them to slap his face. Little Boy Blue wasn't the type to accept death without a fight, but when he realized he was dying, he said, 'God help me through this', kicked a heavy oaken table across the room and fell dead.

Another lieutenant in the house took over his platoon, but as Private Corrigan recorded in 1945, 'our leader was dead and our spirit died with him'.[13]

So it ended in France and the young men who had survived reformed to attack into Germany. Audie Murphy, waiting with the rest of the Third, noted: 'One day the leaf buds appear again on the trees; and in the rear area, where we have been stationed since the fall of the Colmar Pocket, French villagers begin spading their gardens. The men grow restless. With an uneasy eye, they watch the coming of spring. They see the fields drying in the warm winds and know that the ground will soon be ready to support armor.'[14]

Murphy noted too that 'Hope and fear walk hand in hand. We can see the end now, but we are going back up. And always in a man's mind is that one lead pill, that one splinter of steel, that can lose him the race with the finish line in sight.'[15]

'Each of these men wanted desperately to live because of something like the picture in his wallet that constantly reminded him a child was relying on him,' Private Corrigan wrote in 1945. 'Yet time and time again these same men made the decision to sacrifice their lives because it was their duty. In making that decision they resolved that death with their faces in the mud and a bullet through their heads was not the future they wanted for their children. They don't want granite memorials and sweet words; they want peace. Although many of them might not know what UN means, they died for its success.'[16]

Forty years later Mister Kevin Corrigan could write on the same subject to the author: 'Our glory is not our GNP. We can and should be proud of the accomplishment it represents. But it is not, in the current cliché, the bottom line. We must recognize, I feel, that we are a community of free citizens whose freedom has been won and defended by brave men and women. . . . It is something which goes far beyond the cash nexus. The only "price" which can be attached to the Last Full Measure* is the one set specifically by Lincoln: *that we resolve that these dead shall not have died in vain.*'[17]

---

* The name Private Corrigan gave to his tribute to 'Little Boy Blue'.

Epilogue

'Life, to be sure, is nothing much to lose.
But young men think it is, and we were young.'
A. E. Housman

In the autumn of 1945, the best-selling Scots author A. J. Cronin, who prior to the Second World War had made a fortune with his shrewd mixture of sentiment and cynicism, made his first trip to Europe since 1939. Canny Scot that he was, he had carefully removed himself and his family to the United States before the start of the war.

Now he visited war-torn Normandy where he made the acquaintance of a Madame Delnotte at a little inn, the *Lion Rouge*, near Avranches. Intrigued by the cryptic words 'Johnnie Brown, G.I. stays here', scrawled on the door of his bedroom, he asked Madame who 'Johnnie' was. She told him that Johnnie had been an American infantryman who had briefly stayed at the *auberge* before being sent to the front. At that time he had promised the Frenchwoman faithfully that he would come and visit her after the war. Dr Cronin assumed that Johnnie had not come back to visit the Frenchwoman.

'So Johnnie didn't come back?' he asked casually.

'Oh, but yes,' Madame said. 'In fact, he is quite near here. We go to visit him often. For that matter, we go tomorrow.'

'May I come with you?' Cronin asked.

But, of course, Johnnie Brown was long dead, one of the men resting for ever in the great military cemetery at St James.

According to Cronin, the arch sentimentalist. 'Madame Delnotte's expression, usually so contained, had broken – her lips were trembling. . . . Her voice fell almost to a whisper. "He was killed," she said, "by a land mine . . . near Muhlhausen. . . . Johnnie stays with us . . . for ever." Her eyes were wet with tears. "We'll never forget them . . . *never!* . . . Johnnie and those other dear, brave boys . . . for what they did for us . . . for France . . . and for the world."'

Appropriately enough at that moment – for 'Johnnie GI' had apparently loved and tended injured thrushes during his stay at the *auberge* – Cronin heard something. 'Was it my fancy? Suddenly and clearly, in a distant hedgerow, or perhaps it was only in my heart . . . I heard the singing of a thrush.'[1]

Naturally, in spite of the good doctor's sentimental assurances, clearly meant to appeal to his post-war American readers, 'Johnnie GI', killed in the last days of the battle for the Colmar Pocket, and all the rest of the young men who died with him in 1945, are long forgotten in France. Forty years on, there are few signs that they were ever here; of their effort, their determination and misery; of their final sacrifice. The most obvious one is the big US military cemetery on the tree-covered hill overlooking Epinal, where the dead of the Seventh Army are buried. There, stretching as far as the eye can see, are the white crosses, bearing dates in January and February, 1945, of those who died to liberate *la belle France*.

The French, it seems, have long forgotten that debt of blood – a tablet in Colmar, a street name in Nancy, a few battered Maginot Line bunkers along the country road to Neuf-Brisach, shallow depressions in the woods above Wingen, which were once the foxholes in which the scared young men of the 70th Division had quaked during their initiation into combat that January – not much. French nationalism and devotion to *la gloire française* will not allow them to acknowledge any debt to the Americans.

The one Frenchman who knew best of all how much his native France owed to the United States, General Leclerc, the maverick commander of the 2nd French Armoured Division, lived scarcely two years after the war. In 1947 he was killed in a mysterious air crash in North Africa. Some said it was the work of the communists who hated him. But nothing could be proved, for his body was never found.

When his old corps commander, General Wade Haislip, went to visit his widow to express his condolences, Madame Leclerc walked silently over to the fireplace of her drawing room. There she picked up a fire-blackened piece of silver from the Legion of Honour which de Gaulle had presented to her husband that proud day in Colmar.

'Voilà – *Leclerc!*' she said simply, displaying it to the American.[2] That was all they ever found of the headstrong commander of the *2me Division Blindée*.

Yet, ironically, the one Frenchman who really knew what America had done for his poor country, indirectly involved the United States in what was, perhaps, its greatest disaster of the second half of the 20th century – Vietnam.

Fernand Brandel, the French historian, has written that history is like a river. On the surface it flows rapidly and disappears. But down below there is a deeper stream which moves more slowly. But this latter is the more important level because it drives the *whole* river. The surface is time and is not so important. The lower level is continuity and truth. Looking back now from the perspective of the eighties, we can ascertain this lower level, which stretches back to Leclerc's anger at his fellow soldiers of the French Army and the humiliations under their command during Operation Northwind. For the rest of his short life, it seems, Leclerc was determined that the glory of France would be maintained in spite of everything. His first aim was to reform the French Army at home and in North Africa. Never again would it be disgraced as it had been in 1940: a disgrace which had turned him into a fugitive from his own countrymen with a death sentence hanging over his head. But that wasn't to be. De Gaulle, eager to retrieve France's lost colonies, upon which he suspected Britain and America had designs, ordered Leclerc to Indo-China. There, in 1940, the French Vichy Government had allowed the Japanese to set up those bases which they had used for their operations against Burma and Malaya. Now Indo-China was held by a single British division, whose commander, General Gracey, had put down the first Viet Minh revolt on his own initiative and without permission from the Supreme Commander, Mountbatten. On 21 September, 1945, the tough British commander of the 26th Indian Division proclaimed martial law throughout southern Indo-China. Two days later he backed the French *coup d'état* in Saigon.

'Your General Gracey has saved French Indo-China,' a grateful Leclerc told Mountbatten when he met him a little later. Mountbatten was not so pleased. He urged Leclerc not to fight the natives, but to give them their independence if they wanted it. Leclerc, mindful of France's earlier disgraces, would have none of it. According to his aide, Colonel Chatel, Leclerc told Mountbatten that 'he was a soldier and he had come out to fight and fight he would'.[3]

On 5 October, 1945, Leclerc entered Saigon to the cheers of its 10,000 citizens of French extraction, who had profited well from the Japanese, but who were now patriotic Frenchmen once more. Back in Paris, a satisfied de Gaulle noted: 'In Indo-China France was now appearing with suitable dignity.'[4] It was the lull before the storm. Just before Christmas, 1945, Ho Chi Minh and the future General Giap attacked. The long bloody struggle for Indo-China had begun.

Leclerc's son was killed in the fighting, which increased in savagery month by month. Back in France the popular mood was against the war. Leclerc realized that his handful of troops could do little against the well-organized guerrilla army. He sent Chatel to appeal personally to Devers and Haislip for the modern arms and equipment his men so desperately needed. But, as General Haislip recorded later: 'With all the good will in the world, there was just nothing we could do.'⁵

But when another old comrade-in-arms of Leclerc's became president of the United States, the American attitude to Indo-China changed. The first of those 'advisers' were sent to help the hard-pressed French. The 'Quiet Americans', whom Graham Greene noted that year in Saigon, made their appearance and slowly and inevitably America was dragged into that dirty war. Whether President Eisenhower liked it or not, the US Army was being committed in Indo-China.

On 8 March, 1965, with the French long gone now, but with the fighting still raging in what was called Vietnam, a single battalion of US Marines splashed ashore at Da Nang. Before it was all over ten years later, a whole American army would have been involved and 58,000 Americans would have died.

Just as when a stone is thrown into a pond, the ripples spread out with no apparent purpose until they reach the bank, so that deadly 'splash' occasioned by Operation Northwind in 1945 ended thirty years later. And once again young American soldiers paid the price – with their blood.

SOURCE NOTES

A Call to Arms

1 K. Strong, *Intelligence at the Top*, Doubleday, New York, 1969
2 R. Merriam, *Dark December*, Ziff Davis, Chicago, 1947
3 D. Eisenhower, *Crusade in Europe*, Doubleday, New York, 1968
4 ibid.
5 C. Codman, *Drive*, Little, Brown & Co, Boston, 1957
6 Eisenhower, op. cit.
7 D. Irving, *The War Between the Generals*, St. Martins, New York, 1981
8 ibid.
9 Eisenhower, op. cit.
10 M. Shulman, *Defeat in the West*, Ballantine, New York, 1947
11 Reader's letter, *Sunday Telegraph*, 23 Dec, 1984
12 Shulman, op. cit.
13 L. Farago, *Patton*, Obolensky, New York, 1964
14 J. Ellis, *Cassino*, McGraw-Hill, New York, 1984
15 *Report of Operations: The Seventh United States Army in France and Germany 1944–45*, Washington, 1968
16 Eisenhower, op. cit.
17 *The Seventh United States Army in France and Germany, 1944–45*
18 J. Nobecourt, *Hitler's Last Gamble*, Tower, New York, 1980
19 ibid.
20 F. Gilbert, *Hitler Directs His War*, Charter, New York, 1967
21 *The Seventh United States Army in France and Germany, 1944–45*

PART I: Attack!

Chapter One

1 *Combat History of the 324th Infantry Regiment, 44th Infantry Division*, Army Navy Pub Co., Baton Rouge, 1946
2 Combat History 44th Infantry Division, 1944–1945, Albert Love Enterprises, Atlanta, 1946

3 Quoted in J. Toland, *Battle*, New American Library, New York, 1958
4 D. Pence and E. Petersen, *Ordeal in the Vosges*, Transition Press, Sanford 1981
5 W. Cheves, "L'operation Nordwind et Wingen-Sur Moder," manuscript, 1978
6 ibid.
7 J. Carter, *The History of 14th Armored Division*, Albert Love Enterprises, Atlanta, 1946
8 ibid.
9 D. Pence, *Recollections of Philippsbourg*, *Trailblazer* Magazine, November, 1976
10 *History of the 157th Infantry Regiment*, 4 June 1943–8 May 1945, Army Navy Pub. Co., Baton Rouge, 1946
11 W. Munsell, *The Story of a Regiment, A History of the 179th Regimental Combat Team*, Newsfoto Pub. Co., San Angelo, 1946
12 ibid.
13 M. Bass, *The Story of the Century*, Century Association, New York, 1946
14 ibid.
15 ibid.

Chapter Two
1 P. Clostermann, *The Big Show*, Corgi, London, 1952
2 Eisenhower, op. cit.
3 ibid.
4 De Lattre, *The French First Army*, Allen & Unwin, London, 1952
5 De Gaulle, *War Memoirs: Salvation*, Simon & Schuster, New York, 1960
6 ibid.
7 ibid.
8 Pence, op. cit.
9 ibid.
10 ibid.
11 Letter to author
12 Pence, op. cit.
13 Letter to author
14 Cheves, op. cit.
15 ibid.
16 Munsell, op. cit.
17 Letter to author
18 Pence, *Ordeal in the Vosges*
19 De Lattre, op. cit.
20 K. Summersby, *Eisenhower Was My Boss*, Ballantine, 1948
21 De Gaulle, op. cit

22 J. Ellis, *Cassino*
23 D. Irving, *War Among the Generals*
24 ibid.

Chapter Three
1 Cheves, op. cit
2 ibid.
3 Pence, *Ordeal in the Vosges.*
4 ibid.
5 ibid.
6 ibid.
7 ibid.
8 H. Maule, *Out of the Sand*, Corgi, London, 1966
9 ibid.
10 ibid.
11 ibid.
12 ibid.
13 Irving, op. cit.
14 De Gaulle, op. cit.
15 *Medal of Honor Recipients*, US Government Printing Office, Washington, 1973
16 Letter to author
17 Cheves, op. cit.
18 *Stars and Stripes*, February, 1945

Chapter Four
1 Cheves, op. cit.
2 ibid.
3 Letter to author
4 Letter to author
5 Cheves, op. cit.
6 ibid.
7 ibid.
8 W. Cheves, *Snow Ridges and Pill boxes, A True History of the 274th Infantry Regiment of the 70th Division in World War II*, n.p., 1946
9 ibid.
10 ibid.
11 ibid.
12 ibid.
13 ibid.
14 Letter to author
15 Cheves, *Snow Ridges and Pill boxes*
16 Cheves, "*L'operation Nordwind . . .*"
17 ibid.

18 Letter to author
19 Cheves, "*L'operation Nordwind . . .*"
20 ibid.
21 De Lattre, op. cit.
22 Pence, op. Cit.

PART II: Crisis

Chapter One
 1 R. Manvell & H. Fraenkel, *Himmler*, NEL, London, 1965
 2 ibid.
 3 *History of the United States Twelfth Armored Division*, privately printed, Germany, 1945
 4 *The Cross of Lorraine*, privately printed, Germany, 1945
 5 ibid.
 6 ibid.
 7 Pence, op. cit.
 8 ibid.
 9 ibid.
10 ibid.
11 ibid.
12 Cheves, "*L'operation Nordwind . . .*"
13 ibid.
14 ibid.
15 ibid.
16 ibid.
17 Letter to author
18 Cheves, "*L'operation Nordwind . . .*"
19 ibid.
20 Eisenhower, op. cit.
21 P. Leslie, *Anvil*, Hamlyn, London, 1983
22 ibid.
13 Noblecourt, op. cit.
24 De Lattre, op. cit.
25 ibid.

Chapter Two
 1 *The Cross of Lorraine*
 2 Cheves, *Snow Ridges and Pill boxes*
 3 ibid.
 4 Letter to author
 5 Letter to author
 6 Letter to author

7 Letter to author
8 Cheves, *"L'operation Nordwind . . ."*
9 ibid.
10 ibid.
11 ibid.
12 Letter to author
13 Letter to author
14 Cheves, *"L'operation Nordwind . . ."*
15 ibid.
16 ibid.
17 ibid.

Chapter Three
1 Pence, op. cit.
2 ibid.
3 ibid.
4 ibid.
5 Cheves, *"L'operation Nordwind . . ."*
6 ibid.
7 De Lattre, op. cit.
8 D. Taggart, *History of the Third Infantry Division,* Infantry Journal Press, Washington, 1947
9 A. Murphy, *To Hell and Back,* Henry Holt, New York, 1949
10 ibid.
11 S. Ambrose, *The Supreme Commander,* Doubleday, New York, 1970
12 ibid.
13 ibid.
14 ibid.
15 Munsell, op. cit.
16 ibid.
17 J. Hasson, *With the 114th in the E.T.O., A Combat History . . . as Compiled from the Official Historical Records.* Army Navy Pub. Co., Baton Rouge, 1946
18 ibid.
19 Ambrose, op. cit.
20 ibid.

Chapter Four
1 *The Cross of Lorraine*
2 Letter to author
3 Carter, op. cit.
4 ibid.
5 ibid.

6 ibid.
7 ibid.
8 *The Cross of Lorraine*
9 Letter to author
10 Pence, op. cit.
11 *The Seventh United States Army in France and Germany, 1944–45*

PART III: Withdrawal

Chapter One
1 De Lattre, op. cit.
2 ibid.
3 ibid.
4 ibid.
5 *The Fighting Forty-Fifth, The Combat Record of an Infantry Division,* Army Navy Pub. Co., Baton Rouge, 1946
6 *History of the 157th Infantry Regiment*
7 ibid.
8 ibid.
9 Carter, op. cit.
10 ibid.
11 ibid.
12 ibid.
13 *History of the United States 12th Armored Division*
14 *9te und 10te Pz Divisionen,* Munin Verlag, Osnabruck, 1980
15 Carter, op. cit.
16 ibid.
17 ibid.
18 ibid.
19 *The Cross of Lorraine*
20 *The Seventh United States Army in France and Germany, 1944–45*
21 *History of 14th Armored Division*

Chapter Two
1 *The Fighting Forty-Fifth*
2 *History of the 157th Regiment*
3 ibid.
4 *The Fighting Forty-Fifth*
5 *Kampf unter dem Nordlicht,* Munin Verlag. Osnabruck, 1969
6 *History of the 157th Infantry Regiment*
7 *The Fighting Forty-Fifth*
8 *History of the 157th Infantry Regiment*

9 R. Mueller and J. Turk, *Report After Action, The Story of the 103rd Infantry Division*, Wagner'sche Universitats-Buchdruckerei, 1945
10 ibid.
11 Pence, op. cit.
12 ibid.
13 Carter, op. cit.
14 ibid.
15 *Furnace and Fire*, Vienna, Austria, 1945
16 ibid.
17 Ambrose, op. cit.
18 ibid.
19 ibid.
20 ibid.
21 De Lattre, op. cit.
22 ibid.
23 ibid.
24 ibid.

Chapter Three
1 *Furnace and Fire*
2 ibid.
3 ibid.
4 *History of the 103rd Division*
5 ibid.
6 ibid.
7 *The Seventh United States Army in France and Germany*
8 William Huie, *The Execution of Private Slovik*, Delacorte, New York, 1954 and 1970
9 ibid.
10 ibid.
11 ibid.
12 ibid.
13 ibid.
14 ibid.
15 ibid.

PART IV: Counterattack!

Chapter One
1 De Lattre, op. cit.
2 ibid.
3 ibid.
4 Taggart, op. cit.

5 R. Prohme *History of 30th Infantry Regiment, World War II*, Infantry Journal Press, Washington, 1947

6 ibid.

7 ibid.

8 N. White, *From Fedala to Berchtesgaden, A History of the Seventh United States Infantry in World War II*, Keystone Printers, Brocton, 1947

9 A. Murphy, op. cit.

10 ibid.

11 Taggart, op. cit.

12 ibid.

13 ibid.

14 Murphy, op. cit.

15 Hendin & Haas, *Wounds of War*, Basic Books, New York, 1984

16 H. Maule, op. cit.

17 ibid.

18 ibid.

19 ibid.

20 ibid.

21 ibid.

Chapter Two

1 De Lattre, op. cit.

2 ibid.

3 ibid.

4 *BBC War Report*, Collins, London, 1946

5 *History of The United States Twelfth Armored Division*

6 H. Scott, *The Blue and White Devils,* Battery Press, Nashville, 1980

7 De Lattre, op. cit.

8 ibid.

9 ibid.

10 ibid.

11 *History of The United States Twelfth Armored Division*

12 ibid.

13 White, op. cit.

14 Murphy, op. cit.

15 ibid.

16 ibid.

Chapter Three

1 De Lattre, op. cit.

2 ibid.

3 ibid.

4 ibid.
5 Ambrose, op. cit.
6 De Lattre, op. cit.
7 ibid.
8 Ambrose, op. cit.
9 J. Gavin, *On to Berlin*, Bantam, New York, 1978
10 K. Corrigan, *The Last Full Measure, Atlantic Monthly*, 1946
11 ibid.
12 ibid.
13 ibid.
14 Murphy, op. cit.
15 ibid.
16 Corrigan, op. cit.
15 Letter to author

Epilogue

1 A. J. Cronin, *Adventures in Two Worlds,* Little, Brown; Boston, 1956
2 Maule, op. cit.
3 P. Ziegler, *Mountbatten*, Knopf, New York, 1985
4 Maule, op. cit.
5 ibid.

INDEX